SPECIAL EDUCATIONAL NEEDS IN SCHOOLS

Sally Beveridge

London and New York

First published 1993
by Routledge
11 New Fetter Lane

Simultaneously published in the USA and Canada
by Routledge
29 West 35th Street, New York, NY 10001

© 1993 Sally Beveridge

Typeset in Garamond by Witwell Ltd, Southport
Printed and bound in Great Britain by
T.J. Press (Padstow) Ltd, Padstow Cornwall

British Library Cataloguing in Publication Data

A catalogue reference for this book is available from the British Library

ISBN 0-415-07550-5 Hbk
ISBN 0-415-07551-3 Pbk

Library of Congress Cataloging in Publication Data
has been applied for.

ISBN 0-415-07550-5 Hbk
ISBN 0-415-07551-3 Pbk

Contents

Figures

Series editor's foreword

Special educational needs occupy a major but contradictory place in contemporary schooling. Practice in schools and classrooms is ever more comprehensive and sophisticated, but current educational policy is increasingly marginalizing and inhibiting good practice. The special needs allocations within school budgets are being squeezed as LEA formulae are adjusted closer to a raw number pupil recruitment basis; the use of 'unearmarked' funding leaves school budget holders with the temptation of using such monies for other purposes; the devolution of budgets to schools has decimated LEA provided services and centres for SEN; and special schools are facing up to the rigours of Local Management of Schools. Against this background of unstable funding the responsibility and complexity of special needs work in schools continue to grow. As a society we expect more of schools than ever before.

Furthermore, in this calculus of confusion SEN provision must also take account of and adapt to the demands of the National Curriculum and National Testing. The National Curriculum can in one sense be read as a charter of equality for SEN. Students with such needs can no longer be assisgned to a curriculum ghetto which isolates them from their peers and threatens their life chances after school – the National Curriculum is for everybody. On the other hand, the fixed and normative system of pacing which is built into the National Curriculum and the prescription of order and progression in key subjects like mathematics, English and science may effectively remove the flexibility and creativity that is so vital in responding to the individual needs of students with different kinds of learning difficulties. In the same way National Testing and other new test requirements can ensure a continual monitoring of special educational needs. But they can also lead to increased stress upon and competition between students, and result in students with learning difficulties being humiliated and stigmatized. The move towards the use of more traditional 'pen and paper' testing (and traditional forms of examination at GCSE) may well reduce the possibilities that SEN students now have to show what they are capable of. Finally, in the context of published league tables, open enrolment and roll-related budgets, the recruitment of and provision for SEN students takes on an entirely new dimension. The pressure will be on over-subscribed schools to turn away SEN applicants and schools with SEN students may think seriously about spending a greater proportion of their budget on those students who will do well in National Tests. This is the backdrop to Sally Beveridge's careful account of current provision and practice for special educational needs. This is a detailed and comprehensive introduction to the issues, problems and developments in the field. It provides a balanced and insightful survey of classroom, school, LEA and national policies and practice.

Stephen J Ball
Series editor

Acknowledgements

My thanks go to David Sugden, Gordon Whalley and Patrick Wiegand for the encouraging comments and constructive criticism which supported me in writing this book. I am also grateful to Susan Cain, Stuart Hemingway and Phil Jackson for allowing me to use their examples of current school policy and assessment practice.

1 The concept of special educational need

All children can be regarded as having special needs of some kind during their school careers, and there are few of us who, when looking back at our own time as pupils, cannot recollect particular instances where we experienced difficulties in learning or in social contexts. This does not imply, however, that we were necessarily judged by our teachers to be in need of special educational help. For this to have happened, we would have to have been among a minority of pupils whose difficulties were assessed as significantly different from those of their peers. The criteria for such an assessment, and the resulting proportions of pupils who are so identified, have fluctuated over time, for the concept of special educational need is socially constructed. As such, it changes over time in a way which is influenced both by prevalent expectations about children's educational progress and also by political and economic concerns.

The present concept of special educational need is based on the deliberations of the Warnock Committee, which had a governmental brief to investigate and make recommendations about special educational provision, and which published its report in 1978 (DES 1978). The Committee brought together and articulated the views that were current among many of those who were working in special education, and it was generally held to represent a major development in official thinking about special educational need. Although not all of its recommendations have been adopted, it has been of lasting significance, not least because of its insistence that special educational need and special educational provision are central concerns for all who are involved in education, rather than subjects for specialist interest only.

Background to the Warnock recommendations

Prior to the publication of the Warnock Report, need for special educational 'treatment' was associated with the notion of 'disability of mind or body'. The 1944 Education Act had defined eleven categories of disability. These excluded a group of children who were deemed 'ineducable' on account of the severity of their handicaps, but included varying degrees of blindness or deafness, physical impairment, speech defects, educational 'subnormality' and 'maladjustment'. It may be noted that, apart from the latter two categories, disabilities were described in medical terms and their diagnosis appeared to be relatively clear-cut. Educational subnormality and maladjustment were more difficult to determine, implying as they did some value judgements about the cut-off point between 'normal' and 'abnormal' levels of individual variation in learning and in social and emotional development. As these were to become by far the largest of the categories described in the legislation, concerns were increasingly raised about the appropriateness of their definition, particularly as it was found that diagnosis seemed to be associated with certain ethnic and social class variables. Concerns were also voiced that, no matter how severe their impairments, no children should be regarded as ineducable. This argument gathered considerable support, and in 1970 legislation was introduced whereby LEAs were required to make special educational provision for all types of disability. Although it was not stipulated that this provision should necessarily take the form of separate schools or classes, this became the predominant practice and, as a result, 'special education' tended to be regarded as that which occurred in special schools.

Warnock's approach

The Warnock Committee took a much wider view of special education. Drawing attention to the significant numbers of children in ordinary schools who at some time experience difficulties in their learning, it argued that it was not helpful to think in terms of a dichotomy between their educational needs and those of the pupils in special schools. Rather, it wished to see an acknowledgement of the continuum of individual educational need among all pupils. From this broader perspective, special education could be defined as 'any form of additional help, wherever it is provided . . . to overcome educational difficulty' (DES 1978: para. 1.10).

In extending the scope of special education in this way, the Warnock Committee was not suggesting that large numbers of children in ordinary schools should be regarded as having disabilities. On the contrary, it recommended that the existing categorization of disability was educationally inappropriate and should be abolished. It pointed out that to categorize children in such a way could be stigmatizing and, further, that to describe a child as having a particular disability was of little help when it came to determining what sort of educational provision might best meet the child's needs. Children quite frequently have more than one form of difficulty, and that which is most significant from a medical point of view is not necessarily of the greatest educational relevance. Further, there is wide individual variation between the educational needs of children who have the same form of disability, and an undue focus on their impairment may distract attention from other important influences on their learning. The Committee proposed, therefore, that instead of the previous categories a generic term of 'learning difficulties' should be applied to embrace all those pupils who, for whatever reasons, require additional educational help. Figure 1.1 shows three dimensions of learning difficulty that are described in the Warnock Report. From this it can be seen that special educational needs might be long-lasting or short term, specific to particular aspects of learning or more general, and will also vary in the degree to which they affect a child's learning. In recognition of this variation, the Warnock Committee suggested that learning difficulties could be further described as 'mild', 'moderate', 'severe' or 'specific'.

It has frequently been noted that by making this suggestion, rather than abolishing categorization, the Committee effectively provided the basis for a new method of categorizing educational needs. While this has indeed proved to be the case, it does not detract from the importance of the Committee's arguments for a shift away from a medical model of children's learning

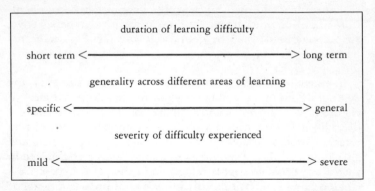

Figure 1.1 Dimensions of learning difficulty in Warnock's continuum of special educational need

difficulties. Its line of reasoning represents an explicit attempt to break with traditional notions of educational difficulty as being primarily rooted and fixed within the individual child. It did not deny that within-child factors can have a significant impact on learning, but the concept of special educational need which was put forward was far more concerned with the *interaction* between the child and the learning contexts which the child experiences. An interactive explanation of educational need has, as the Committee argued, many more positive implications for schools than are offered by the traditional model. It allows us to view children's needs as a result of a mismatch between the knowledge, skills and experiences they bring to their learning situations and the demands that are made of them. From this perspective, there are constructive steps that can be taken to overcome or even prevent learning difficulties.

The principle that children's special educational needs cannot be viewed in isolation from the learning contexts in which they arise is further emphasized by the three aspects of need that are identified in the Warnock Report:

(i) the provision of special means of access to the curriculum;
(ii) the provision of a special or modified curriculum;

(iii) particular attention to the social structure and emotional climate in which education takes place.

(DES 1978: para. 3.19)

The first of these provisions is not controversial. Where children have difficulties which prevent them from gaining access to the curriculum in the usual way, then clearly they need whatever help is necessary to allow them to participate as fully as possible in the learning experiences that are provided. For example, children with sensory or physical impairments may need special equipment or attention to positioning, and others may benefit from the use of adapted materials. The second and third provisions have given rise to rather more debate, however. Though not denying that the curriculum and the social and emotional climate are important influences on children's learning, some (e.g. Galloway 1985) have suggested that children may too readily be transferred to different curricular activities and social groupings, and that there is no guarantee that this will help them overcome their difficulties. They point out that the 'ordinary' curriculum and climate for learning in schools may add to as well as alleviate children's difficulties, and argue that the better these are matched to the needs of all pupils then the less likelihood there will be that substantial numbers of children will be regarded as having needs which require special educational provision.

The fact that there is considerable variation between schools in the proportion of their pupils who experience educational difficulties is not in doubt. Indeed an acceptance of the interactive nature of special educational needs implies an acknowledgement of their relativity. Thus, a child who is identified as having learning difficulties in one school would not automatically be judged in the same way in another. The child's needs, therefore, can be seen to be relative to those of the other pupils in the school, the teachers' knowledge, skills and approach, the school's approach to individual diversity, LEA policy and so on. Given this relativity, it is not surprising to find that estimates of the prevalence of special educational needs are problematic. On the basis of the research evidence that was available, the Warnock Committee estimated that as many as 20 per cent of pupils might have such needs at some point in their school career and, although certain reservations have been voiced, this figure has generally been accepted.

The implications of the Warnock Committee's approach

In summing up the Warnock Committee's approach to the concept of special educational needs, it would be fair to say that it was representative of the opinions of many of those who were involved in special education at the time. Among these professionals, there was a large degree of acceptance of the notion that the scope of special education should be conceived much more broadly, and that a continuum of special educational needs, with particular attention to their interactive and relative nature, should be recognized. The new concept did, though, have wide-ranging and major implications for ordinary schools and their teachers. Previously, it had been possible to see special education as separate from the ordinary school system. Where significant learning difficulties were experienced by pupils in ordinary classes, there were channels for referring these pupils for special help elsewhere. If one in five pupils were to be regarded as having such difficulties, however, then it became apparent that special education must be conceived as an integral part of the whole educational system. Fewer than 2 per cent of pupils have traditionally been educated in separate special provision and therefore the vast majority of pupils with special educational needs have been educated in ordinary schools. It follows that all teachers must now be seen to have a responsibility for making special educational provision for those pupils experiencing learning difficulties in their classes. Furthermore, the acknowledgement of the interactive and relative nature of those pupils' needs makes it clear that both teachers individually and schools collectively have a significant role to play in alleviating or adding to their difficulties. In order to explore the nature of that role, it is necessary to look more closely at the implications of the main features of the Warnock Committee's concept of special educational need.

The interactive nature of special educational need

Most teachers would accept, at least in principle, that the educational difficulties which children experience can only be fully understood by reference to the contexts in which they arise. Although it is clear that some children have cognitive limitations or other impairments that may impede their progress, it is also generally acknowledged that there can be very different educational outcomes for such children. Among the complex and interacting factors that contribute to this diversity, it is probable that the attitudes and expectations of others, and the type of support, knowledge and understanding that they experience at home, at school and in their local community, all play a significant part.

Few teachers would need persuading of the importance of home background factors in children's attainment and behaviour at school. For most children home is clearly not only their first and primary learning environment, but one which continues to exert a powerful influence. Further, there is ample research evidence to demonstrate an association between poor educational achievement and measures of social disadvantage (Mortimore and Blackstone 1982), although it should be noted that there are a number of different explanations put forward for this finding. Teachers frequently cite parental attitudes to school and apparent interest in their children's education as critical factors, and certainly the need for good home–school relations was given a high profile in the Warnock Report. In order to foster such relations, however, positive attitudes towards and interest in parental perspectives by schools seem likely to be as important as home background variables.

Recognition of the significant influence of home on attainment at school should not lead to the conclusion that schools themselves have only a subsidiary role to play. It must be acknowledged, though, that the idea that schools can affect the difficulties experienced by some of their pupils may not yet be widespread among teachers. For example, in a study of special educational needs in junior schools, Croll and Moses (1985) asked teachers for their explanation of the needs of children in their classes. The vast majority of references were to 'within-child' factors for those with learning difficulties, and to home background for those with emotional or behavioural difficulties. Mention of school-based factors was made in fewer than 4 per cent of all cases. However, the evidence from research in schools at both primary and secondary levels (Mortimore *et al.* 1988, Rutter *et al.* 1979) does suggest that schools vary in effectiveness in educating pupils even when they come from similar home backgrounds and have similar initial levels of achievement. The schools which were judged to be effective in these studies were able to raise both overall levels of attainment and also general standards of behaviour. As Galloway (1985) has pointed out, this does not imply that they would not still be able to identify a number of their pupils whose achievements were less advanced. This will be true of any school, regardless of its overall standards. Although it could be argued that the more effective the school, the fewer of its pupils are likely to need special help, it is probable that the criteria for determining what constitutes 'learning difficulty' will shift according to changes in general levels and expectations of achievement.

The scope of special educational needs

In their survey of junior schools Croll and Moses (1985) found that, on average, class teachers judged 18.8 per cent of their pupils to have some form of special educational need. As under 2 per cent of pupils remain in special schools, this might be taken as strong support for Warnock's estimate. However, it has been argued that the figure of 20 per cent has become a target (e.g. Ainscow and Muncey 1989) and that given the expectation that there will be this proportion of pupils experiencing difficulties, schools have begun to identify a group of their lowest achieving pupils accordingly. This is perhaps a rather over-simplified interpretation, as all the evidence suggests considerable variation between schools in the numbers of pupils judged to have special educational needs. It is undoubtedly the case, though, that the identification of need may often be more influenced by the educational criteria currently in use than by an individual pupil's characteristics, and for this reason not all have welcomed the way in which the scope of special education has been broadened. Their concerns focuses both on which children are identified as in need, and also on what follows from their identification.

Sociologists of education such as Tomlinson (1981, 1982) have drawn attention to the disproportionate representation of 'relatively powerless groups in society' in those special schools that cater for pupils with moderate learning difficulties and emotional and behavioural difficulties. Tomlinson has argued that factors of socio-economic and ethnic status are significantly associated with the identification of these forms of special educational need, and that as the scope of special education expands within ordinary schools so larger and larger numbers of children from the lowest status families will be judged to have such difficulties.

Most of those concerned with special education would accept the evidence that social factors are involved in the identification of special educational need. Indeed, the influence of gender, as well as of socio-economic class and ethnicity, has frequently been documented. There is rather more debate, however, about the impact of identification on the pupils concerned. The Warnock Committee made it quite clear that it saw identification as a positive first step for any pupil who was experiencing difficulties. It recommended that all schools should have procedures which enable them to identify pupils as early as possible, so that special help can be given both to enable pupils to overcome their current difficulties and, hopefully, to prevent more serious difficulties from arising subsequently. By contrast, Tomlinson, while not denying the importance of such 'humanitarian' motives for the identification of special educational need, argues that historically it has often served a different purpose. She suggests that, rather than being primarily concerned with the needs of individuals, special education has traditionally acted as a 'safety valve' for the ordinary education system, by removing those pupils who posed a challenge to its smooth operation. As a result, an extensive specialist and separate service has grown up with a focus on individual difficulties, and this has served to distract attention from what might be problematic in the ordinary school system. Furthermore, whether pupils have been removed to different groups in ordinary schools or to special schools, they have typically been provided with different curricular experiences. Tomlinson concludes that these are of lower status than the ordinary school curriculum, and that this, in conjunction with lowered expectations of the pupils, is likely to lead to the poor progress that is taken to justify the initial assessment of educational difficulty. Thus, given that most of the pupils come from low status families, she characterizes special education as a form of 'social control'.

Not surprisingly, Tomlinson's position has proved to be controversial. Cole (1989), for example, maintains that her historical perspective is selective. Although he accepts that the social control hypothesis has some substance, he puts forward an alternative analysis which leads him to conclude that humanitarian motives have been far more influential in the development of special education than Tomlinson implies. Nevertheless, her arguments have been particularly important in their emphasis that the needs of individual children cannot be viewed in isolation from the wider social context in which they occur. At the school level, children who are experiencing learning or emotional and behavioural difficulties may show up weaknesses in the existing approach. If as many as one in five have such difficulties, then rather than seeking reasons for this within the individuals themselves, the solution may lie in changes to the curriculum and organization of the school. This perspective can be summarized by Galloway's observation:

> The question is whether a curriculum and emotional climate which fails to cater for up to 20 per cent of pupils can be entirely suitable for the remaining 80 per cent.
>
> (Galloway 1985: 6)

The continuum of educational need

The notion of a continuum of educational need was fundamental to the Warnock Committee's thinking. The traditional view of discrete categories of pupils, made up of those who require special educational help and those who do not, served not only to emphasize differences rather than similarities between children, but also to distract attention from the diversity of individual need that all can experience in their learning. Among teachers, the recognition of such diversity may be reflected in the scepticism some demonstrate when they refer to the 'myth of the normal child', or in the more frequently expressed view that 'all children are special'. On the whole this does not, of course, prevent them from making relative judgements about children in which general expectations about 'normal' progress are implicit. Thus, for example, a pupil's attainment may be described as 'above' or 'below' average, and behaviour may be judged to be 'mature' or 'immature'. Those pupils whose attainment and behaviour are significantly poorer than those of their peers will rightly cause their teachers concern. However, what becomes problematic when considering the continuum of children's needs is the question: at what point do individual educational needs become 'special'?

Any cut-off point on a continuum can seem arbitrary and this, coupled with the recognition of the relativity of needs, has led to some uncertainty in decisions about what constitutes special educational need. There are those (e.g. Ainscow and Muncey 1989) who think that we should abandon the term altogether. They believe that, when applied as a label to children, it is just as likely to lead to stigmatization and an exphasis on difference as the former categories of disability that the Warnock Committee sought to replace. For this reason, they argue that it is more appropriate to refer only to 'individual educational needs'. Others, however (e.g. Roaf and Bines 1989), see the concept of special educational need as fundamentally linked to principles of equal opportunities and rights. Children who experience difficulties in their learning may often be afforded low status in schools, particularly when accountability is measured primarily by academic achievement, and this status is likely to affect decisions about resource allocation. Yet these children need additional help if they are to make the most of their educational opportunities. If the necessary resources for this assistance are to be made available, then it seems clear that relevant differences must be identified and acknowledged. As Roaf points out 'To ignore differences altogether, or to pay too much attention to irrelevant differences, are both equally unjust' (Roaf 1989: 93).

From this perspective then, the question of how special educational need differs from other educational need becomes crucial. The possibility of stigma is not denied, for it is only too apparent that any label which is applied to a minority group can acquire derogatory overtones. Unfortunately, however, this may happen with or without the use of officially recognized terminology. Rather than seeking to abandon the label of special educational need, therefore, it may be more effective to tackle any accompanying stigma by explicit attempts to promote an equal valuing of individual diversity. Thus, as Roaf has emphasized, the aims of special education should be seen to embrace not only the needs, rights and opportunities of the children who experience difficulties, but also the attitudes, values and behaviour of their peers.

How special are special educational needs?

The concept of special educational needs that was put forward by the Warnock Committee has added complexity to the question of just how far special educational needs should be regarded as special. The question is, however, an important one for teachers because, as the Committee indicated, they are not only the people who in most cases will identify these needs, but they also have a responsibility for meeting them. Different teachers will be more or less willing to make an early decision that the difficulties an individual pupil is experiencing are significant enough to describe as special. They will be influenced in this by the sorts of argument that have been discussed in this chapter, and also by their feelings of professional competence in responding to diverse individual needs. Furthermore, they may be guided in their decisions by school and LEA policies determining the nature and extent of additional resources to meet identified needs. In practice they are likely to identify those children whom they find most difficult to teach because of poor progress and achievement or problematic behaviour or both.

There is no doubt that children with learning and emotional or behavioural difficulties pose a challenge to teachers, but the extent of their needs will be relative to the quality of the educational experiences with which they are provided. It has often been argued that what is needed by children with special educational needs is good overall educational practice, and there is some evidence to support such a view. The HMI survey of special educational needs in ordinary schools (1989), for example, concluded that the 'features of good practice' that it was able to identify 'applied to the teaching of all pupils, and not just to those with special educational need' (HMI 1989: para. 26).

Certainly, the acceptance of a continuum of need implies that a continuum may also be described in the sort of educational help that children require. From this perspective, special education is not regarded as necessarily being qualitatively different from other education, but rather as different in the degree of assistance and support that may be given. As Fish (1989) has argued, this is neither to deny nor to undervalue the specific expertise of those teachers who work with pupils with severe and specialist needs. It does emphasize, however, that all teachers need to develop their practice and their responsiveness to individual differences in ways which can help children overcome their educational difficulties.

Discussion points

1 'All children are special.' What arguments can be made for and against the proposition that we should move towards a concept of 'individual' rather than 'special' educational needs?

2 'The fact that a child has special needs does not necessarily imply that the child, as an individual, needs help. The most effective way to help the child may be to review aspects of school organisation, or teaching methods and resources' (Galloway 1985). How far does the recognition that special educational needs are both relative and interactive in nature lend support to this perspective?

3 Tomlinson characterizes special educational provision as a form of 'social control'. What concerns do her arguments raise for teachers, and how far are these justified?

Further reading

Galloway, D. (1985) *Schools, Pupils and Special Educational Needs*, London: Croom Helm.
Roaf, C. and Bines, H. (eds) (1989) *Needs, Rights and Opportunities: Developing Approaches to Special Education*, Lewes: Falmer.

2 The legislative framework

The influence of the Warnock Report (DES 1978) was not restricted to a new conceptualization of special educational needs; it also made wide-ranging recommendations about the way in which special educational provision should be developed. The Committee envisaged that this provision should be seen as 'additional or supplementary' rather than 'separate or alternative' to regular education, and described a continuum of settings in which it might take place. For most children, their needs would be met in ordinary classrooms, with additional support as required. In order that their rights to special educational provision were safeguarded, a system for identifying and assessing needs was proposed and, where these could not be met within ordinary school resources, LEAs should draw on the advice of a wide range of professionals in order to determine the appropriate form of additional help. Importantly, parents were to be seen as key participants in the decision-making process. Indeed, an important theme of the Warnock Report was that a *partnership* between schools and parents was crucial to the children's successful education.

The 1981 Education Act*

Many of the Warnock Committee's recommendations were taken up in the 1981 Education Act. The main provisions of this Act are concerned with definitions of special educational need and provision, the role of ordinary schools in meeting special educational needs, the identification and assessment of need and the rights of parents in the decision-making process.

Definitions of special educational need and provision

The previous statutory categories of disability are replaced in the Act by one of special educational need. The definition of special educational needs, as a number of commentators have pointed out, is somewhat circular. That is, a child is to be regarded as having special educational needs if he or she has 'a learning difficulty which calls for special educational provision to be made'. While no further criteria are provided to determine exactly what constitutes this level of difficulty, reference is made to children whose difficulties are 'significantly greater' than experienced by others of the same age, as well as to those with a disability which impedes access to the facilities which are generally provided. Children of below school age who, if they do not receive special help, are thought likely to fall into one of these categories later, are also included in the definition. However, those whose educational difficulties are solely related to the fact that the language used at school is different from that used at home are specifically excluded. As studies by both Fish (ILEA 1985) and Croll and Moses (1985) have suggested, however, it may sometimes be difficult for teachers to make the distinction between the particular needs of those learning in a second or third language and the special educational needs circumscribed in this legislation.

Special educational provision is described as 'additional to, or otherwise different from' that which is generally made for pupils, but the legislation puts a duty on LEAs to ensure that, provided that certain conditions are met, children with special educational needs are educated in ordinary schools. The conditions that are specified allow for a considerable range of interpretation. They are that the views of the child's parents must be taken into account, and that placement in an ordinary school is compatible not only with the child's receiving the special provision required, but also with the effective education of the other pupils there and with the efficient use of resources. It is stipulated that where children are educated in ordinary schools, then they should be involved 'in the activities of the school together with children who do not have special educational needs' (Section 2 (7)). Both LEAs and school governors are charged with responsibilities to keep the arrangements made for meeting special educational needs under review.

Identification and assessment procedures

The Act makes it clear that ordinary schools have a responsibility to identify, assess and provide for the majority of children with special educational needs and to monitor their progress. However, in effect it distinguishes between the sort of continuous assessment that should be an integral part of every school's role, and that which is required in the minority of cases where the education that can be offered within 'generally available' resources is not sufficient to meet a child's needs. When this situation arises, under the provisions of the Act, the LEA must initiate formal statutory assessment procedures in order to determine whether the child's needs are such that additional or special resources should be allocated.

Circular 1/83 (DES 1983a), which provided the initial guidance on these procedures (subsequently updated by Circular 22/89 (DES 1989b)), emphasizes that there are some general principles which should apply to both school-based and LEA assessments. These include the recognition of the interactive nature of special educational needs:

> A child's special educational needs are . . . related to his abilities as well as his disabilities, and to the nature of his interaction with his environment.
>
> (DES 1983a: para. 3)

The Circular also stesses the need for partnership:

> In looking at the child as a whole person, the involvement of the child's parents is essential. Assessment should be seen as a partnership between teachers, other professionals and parents . . . . The feelings and perceptions of the child concerned should be taken into account, and the concept of partnership should wherever possible be extended to older children and young persons.
>
> (DES 1983a: para. 6)

A major criticism that has been made of the 1981 Act is that it says nothing about the form that school-based assessments should take, but the Circular makes it clear that individual LEAs are expected to provide guidance to their schools on the way in which these should be developed. The formal statutory procedures are, however, specified in considerable detail both in the Act and in the 1983 Education (Special Educational Needs) Regulations (DES 1983b).

These should be initiated when the LEA has grounds to believe that additional or special resources will be needed to meet a child's educational needs. Although this should not be the first indication to parents that their child is experiencing difficulties, and indeed they can themselves request an assessment, the LEA must inform them in writing of its intention to begin the procedures. In doing so, it should provide information about what is involved and about the rights of parents to put forward their views. It should also give the name of an LEA officer who can provide them with further details. Parents have at least twenty-nine days to respond, and the LEA must take account of their views in deciding whether or not to proceed. At all stages, parents are to be kept informed of the decisions that are made. When assessment does go ahead, the LEA must seek advice from all relevant professionals, including, for example, those from health and social service departments, as well as from education. Following this, the LEA determines whether there is a case for special provision to be made. If so, it has to draft a statement and send this, together with copies of the professional advice, to the parents.

The draft statement should specify first the precise nature of the child's assessed difficulties and educational needs, and second the provision that the LEA proposes to make in order to meet the child's needs. If parents disagree with part or all of the statement, or with a decision not to draw up a statement, the LEA must consider whether or not to modify its decision. If disagreements still persist, parents have the right of appeal to an Appeals Committee and, beyond that, to the Secretary of State. The expectation, however, is that in the vast majority of cases the lengthy consultative procedures will allow for an assessment to be made of a child's needs which is based on 'an agreed understanding' among all those concerned, and therefore the appeals procedure will not be necessary. Figure 2.1 illustrates the form a statement of special educational need can take. Where statements are drawn up, the Act specifies that they should be reviewed at least annually, and that a reassessment should take place, usually at the age of about thirteen and a half years. Parents are to be informed of any changes which are proposed to their child's statement and also have the right to request the LEA to undertake reassessments.

Response to the 1981 Act

While the 1981 Act introduced some welcome and significant changes to the legislative framework for special educational provision, it was greeted with a certain amount of ambivalence by those who were to be responsible for putting its provisions into effect. The reservations that were expressed fell into two main categories: first, that some of the 'spirit' of the Warnock Committee's recommendations had been lost, and second, that several of the new procedures would prove to be problematic in their implementation.

The official recognition that was given to the interactive nature and scope of special educational need was generally regarded as a positive step, and one which set special education within the mainstream of educational thinking. However, although the influence of the learning environment on children's needs was acknowledged, little attention was paid to the sorts of educational experience that would help children overcome their difficulties. As Fish (1989) has pointed out, the focus was centred more on where children should receive their education than on what they would actually receive. In this respect, too, the Act was disappointing to those who had hoped for a less equivocal stance on the issue of integration. While a duty is placed on LEAs to make special educational provision in ordinary schools, the provisos that are attached to this are sufficient to allow them to maintain their previous approach towards the placement of pupils in separate schools or classes.

The new assessment procedures that were introduced also provoked a great deal of debate. These were designed to

Section I   (specifies details of child's name, date of birth and address; parent's or guardian's name and address)

Section II   Special Educational Needs

'Child X's special needs are:
   to develop spoken language skills;
   to develop basic literacy skills;
   to develop basic numeracy skills;
   to develop concentration span;
   to develop social skills.'*

Section III   Special Educational Provision
              (includes specification of any modification or exception to the National Curriculum)

'Access to the full National Curriculum at an appropriate level as part of a normal class group, with:
1 implementation of programmes to develop communication skills;
2 individual and teacher-directed small group provision to develop literacy skills;
3 individual and teacher-directed small group provision to develop numeracy skills;
4 some in-class support to help child X's access to the curriculum;
5 implementation of programmes to develop concentration span;
6 implementation of programmes to develop social skills;
   (4 to 6 require n hours daily Special Needs Assistant time, provided on a small group basis)
7 close home/school liaison.'*

Section IV   Appropriate School or Other Arrangements
              (specifies type of school and names any particular school which is considered appropriate)

Section V   Additional Non-educational Provision
              (specifies any additional provision such as medical monitoring of hearing, vision, etc. which is needed)

Figure 2.1 An example of the format for a statement of special educational needs

Note:* The examples given in Sections II and III are not verbatim extracts from one child's statement, but are illustrative of the sorts of need and provision that may be specified.

safeguard additional resources for those children with the most evident needs, but Dessent (1987) has argued that they run contrary to the principle of a continuum of need. That is, the focus that they place on a particular minority serves to distract attention from others with special educational needs, and thereby perpetuates traditional notions of categorization. Furthermore, the absence of any clear criteria for decisions about when a statement might be required has led to concerns that the 'agreed understanding' between professionals and parents that is envisaged in the Act may in practice be hard to achieve. Where statements are drawn up, Circular 1/83 emphasizes that there should be a clear distinction between the analysis of a child's difficulties and his or her needs for particular kinds of help, and the specification of the special educational provision that the LEA proposes to make in order to meet these needs. Some predicted, however, that in a time of financial constraint, such a distinction would pose practical problems and that the assessment of need would continue to be strongly influenced by an LEA's existing patterns of special educational provision. Finally, while in principle the process of consultation with parents and with all concerned professionals was generally welcomed, the time-consuming and bureaucratic nature of the new procedures, even when there is agreement about a child's need for additional help, was widely criticized.

There is no doubt that the Act provides for a considerable extension of parental rights to participate in educational decision-making, at least where their children's needs are judged to be sufficiently significant to warrant formal assessment. However, the emphasis that the Warnock Committee had given to parent–professional partnerships is only partly addressed. For example, its recommendation that, following identification of special educational need, a 'named person' should be allocated who could advise and support parents was not taken up. In the absence of such assistance, as many were quick to point out, it was not at all clear how far parents would feel sufficiently informed to exercise their rights.

Other key aspects of the Warnock Report which were not addressed in the 1981 Act also gave rise to concern. Although the Committee had been asked to base its recommendations on the principle of making the most effective use of existing resources, it put forward strong arguments for substantial additional funding in three priority areas if needs were to be adequately met. The areas identified were in services for those under five or over sixteen years old, and in initial and in-service teacher training to increase professional knowledge, skills and understanding of special educational needs. However, no additional funds were forthcoming as a result of the legislation, and it was perhaps the greatest single cause of criticism of the Act that its implementation was to be achieved through the reallocation of existing resources.

The implementation of the 1981 Act

The 1981 Act has been described as an enabling rather than a prescriptive piece of legislation (Welton *et al.* 1982), which sets the framework for special educational provision but allows for a range of interpretation, and thus for considerable diversity in LEA response. As Goacher and his colleagues (1988) have pointed out, any major changes following the legislation were only likely to occur where there was a genuine reappraisal of existing attitudes and ideas, and of the relationships that professionals had with parents and their children. On the basis of their research, they suggest that for some LEAs there has been little change in practice, while for others change has been extensive and wide-ranging. This variability between LEAs will in part have reflected differences in their policies prior to the Act, but it is also an indication that it is possible to follow the letter of the legislation without necessarily subscribing to the spirit of the Warnock Committee's principles upon which the Act was based.

Many LEAs make explicit reference to the interactive and relative nature of special educational needs in their policy statements. An influential review of provision in the Inner London Education Authority (ILEA 1985) set special education clearly within an equal opportunities framework, arguing that there needed to be 'changing attitudes, arrangements and approaches in schools, colleges and the community to minimise inequalities' (1.1.28). It went on to recommend that, wherever possible, both the child or young person and his or her family should be fully involved in planning and decision-making, and that the services which are provided should include the

opportunity not only for early special help but also for continuous interaction with peers who do not have special educational needs. A number of LEAs have in principle accepted these
recommendations as appropriate aims for the development of
their services. At the same time, however, there is evidence that
other authorities maintain distinct categorizations of pupils, and
that the use of initials to identify groups, such as MLD to
represent children with moderate learning difficulties, remains
widespread (Goacher *et al.* 1988).

It might be assumed that differences in the way that LEAs
conceptualize special educational needs will affect their policy
on integration, and certainly there seems to be wide variation in
practice. Some authorities had already initiated integration
schemes prior to the 1981 Act and have continued to develop
these, but the overall national picture is far from clear. Goacher
and his colleagues (1988) detected some indications of a trend
towards an increase in placement in ordinary schools. This does
not imply, however, that they found evidence of a general
breaking down of the boundary between special and ordinary
school provision. On the contrary, they found that in more than
a third of LEAs, statements of special educational need are
withdrawn if children are transferred from special to ordinary
school, thus reinforcing the distinction between the two. Moreover, a comparative survey of LEA practice (Swann 1988a) has
revealed that, whereas some authorities are placing proportionally more children with special educational needs in ordinary
schools, others are increasing their provision in separate schools
and classes.

LEAs also vary with respect to their statementing policies. In
Goacher's study (1988) estimates of the proportions of pupils
for whom statements were maintained varied from less than 1.3
per cent to over 2.7 per cent, and some have suggested that the
real range may be wider, particularly since the implementation
of the 1988 Education Reform Act. Goacher found clear
evidence of considerable variability both in the criteria LEAs
employed in their assessment of need and also in the extent of
the additional resources that they provided. This, coupled with
the finding that the average time taken to complete formal
assessment procedures ranged from twelve to thirty-six weeks

in different authorities, suggests that the degree of satisfaction experienced both by parents and by the professionals involved is also likely to vary.

As far as parental involvement in the continuing assessment process is concerned, both LEA policy and school practice differ with respect to the annual reviews of statements and the re-assessments which take place. Despite this diversity, a clear consensus emerges (e.g. Sandow *et al.* 1987, Vaughan 1989) that neither in the initial assessment nor subsequently do parents feel that they are 'equal partners' with the professionals. While there are a small number of instances of parents using the appeals procedures, and on occasion taking their case beyond the Secretary of State to the law courts, the majority report that they do not feel they have been able to make a significant contribution to the decision-making process.

Reservations about the implementation of the assessment procedures do not only relate to parental involvement. For example, collaboration between education, health and other agencies is fundamental to their operation, but is not always easy to achieve. Furthermore, some educational psychologists have voiced their anxiety that the writing of statements may be as much influenced by resource implications as by the assessment of individual need. Certainly it has been reported that statements are frequently written in general and non-specific terms (Goacher *et al.* 1988).

It should be stressed, however, that despite the practical problems in its implementation, the 1981 Act led to several positive changes. First, there is no doubt that it served to raise general awareness about the range of special educational needs that children may experience, and to place these needs firmly in the context of mainstream educational practice. Furthermore, at least during the early years of its implementation, Gipps, Gross and Goldstein (1987) found evidence to suggest that the Act had resulted in the protection of resources during a time of general financial cut-back. Their study indicated that most LEAs had found a means to maintain or even extend the resources allocated to special educational provision, and, although the ways in which these were deployed varied from authority to authority, they were able to identify some common trends.

Most LEAs have reorganized and redefined the roles of their support services. Thus, whereas previously these may have become involved only with those schools which sought assistance for particular pupils, the service has generally now been extended to all schools in the area. Formerly, direct teaching of individuals or groups of pupils tended to predominate in the work of support services, but increasingly their role has centred on advice and assistance for teachers. A shift can be described then from a model of individualized and pupil-focused 'remediation' by peripatetic staff towards one which emphasizes the need for schools to develop their own approach to meeting all their pupils' needs.

Within schools, a similar change has been seen in the work of those staff who are designated as having a particular responsibility for pupils with special educational needs. Like the authority's support teams, these 'remedial teachers' generally spent most of their time working directly with pupils in separate classes and groups. Frequently they, like the pupils they taught, were reported to hold low status in the school, and the work they did was often somewhat detached from that of their colleagues. However, increasingly some of them have been required to take on a more extensive and central role, which has been characterized as that of 'special needs co-ordinator'. That is, in addition to their direct teaching duties, they have also been given responsibilities to co-ordinate and monitor the learning experiences that are provided for pupils with special educational needs throughout the school. In order to do this effectively, they need not only to liaise with their colleagues but also to provide them with support and advice. Not surprisingly, therefore, in a number of authorities there has been an explicit attempt to ensure that relatively senior and experienced staff are allocated to this position, and that in-service training opportunities have been made available through which they might extend their knowledge and skills.

These changes in the organization of support for pupils with special educational needs are associated with what has become known as the 'whole school approach'. The term implies that special educational provision is an integral part of the work of a school and that all teachers are explicitly regarded as teachers of pupils with special educational needs. They may be supported in their work by designated colleagues and by members of the authority's advisory team, but essentially they retain direct responsibility for meeting their pupils' needs. In practice, this may as yet represent an aim rather than a reality in many schools, for although Gipps and her colleagues found that most teachers accepted the underlying principles, their degree of commitment was strongly influenced by their views on the quality and extent of support that they received. Thus, even within schools which had embraced the aims of the new approach, they found that elements of the traditional remedial model often still remained.

Although not explicitly addressed by the 1981 Act, one further trend since its implementation concerns the interactions that take place between ordinary and special schools. The Warnock Committee had strongly recommended that closer working relationships should be established, and that special schools should be seen as a source of potential support for teachers in ordinary schools. A survey by Jowett, Hegarty and Moses (1988) found that the vast majority of special schools have begun to establish some sort of link with their neighbourhood schools. These initiatives vary in their nature and extent, but where they have been well planned, benefits have been reported for the staff and pupils of both schools. From the evidence of this study it seems clear that such links represent an important way in which notions of 'differentness' may gradually be replaced by a fuller understanding of the continuum of educational need.

The progress that had been made since the 1981 Act as well as the continuing areas for concern were summarized by the House of Commons Select Committee which met in 1987 to review its implementation. This Committee acknowledged that there was still some confusion about the concept of special educational need and that its relativity led to difficulties in decision-making, but overall it reported that the main principles upon which the Act was based had been accepted. It found that special educational provision had become far more integral to the work of ordinary schools than was previously the case, and it felt able to give its full support to the principle of integration.

Indeed, although the Committee was clear that there was a continuing role for special schools, it wished to see LEAs make their stance on integration much clearer in their policy statements. While it felt that a great deal had been achieved, it raised criticisms about the inadequacy of the information and help that was given to parents, and drew attention to the need for clearer guidelines and more streamlined procedures for the drawing up of statements. Importantly, it emphasized that a commitment to extra resources was required if the principles of the Act were to be put fully into practice.

In the same year that the Select Committee presented these findings, however, the Secretary of State for Education introduced detailed and wide-ranging proposals for educational reform which led to considerable apprehension that much of the work of the 1981 Act might be undone. Rather than being integral to the thinking of this 1987 Education Reform Bill, special educational needs were conspicuous by their absence. One reference was made to special schools, and in a further clause it was suggested that children with statements would be exempt from the provisions of the proposed National Curriculum. No mention at all was made of the majority of pupils with special educational needs. The overwhelming response of those involved in special educational provision was that the Bill was incompatible with the principles of the 1981 Act. As a result of extensive lobbying, a number of positive changes were introduced into what became the 1988 Education Reform Act, and these were further reinforced in the circulars of guidance that were issued on its implementation. However, some significant areas for concern remained.

The 1988 Education Reform Act

The 1988 Act introduced a great number of changes to the education system as a whole. In considering its impact on provision for pupils with special educational needs, most attention has been focused on the National Curriculum and associated programme of assessment, and on the devolution of financial management from LEAs to schools.

The National Curriculum

Early fears that a minority of pupils would be automatically
exempted from the National Curriculum subsided when the
DES made it clear that the entitlement to the 'broad and
balanced' curriculum that was envisaged applied to all pupils.
This was generally welcomed, not only because it was in
accordance with principles of equal opportunity, but also
because it emphasized a continuum between ordinary and
special educational provision. There was some optimism that
the entitlement to the National Curriculum might both broaden
and raise the status of the learning experiences that were
provided for pupils with special educational needs. If it were to
do so, however, then it was essential first that the full range of
individual need should be taken into account in drawing up the
curriculum plans and, further, that the implementation of these
plans should be sufficiently flexible to allow maximum
participation by all pupils. Just how far these conditions have
been met remains open to debate.

Some have argued that had the full range of needs been
considered from the beginning the current emphasis on the
subject-based nature of the National Curriculum would have
been balanced by more explicit attention to cross-curricular
dimensions and personal and social education. Both of these
have been described as important areas of curriculum planning
for pupils with special educational needs and, while their
significance has been acknowledged in principle by the DES, it
remains the case that the most detailed National Curriculum
guidance for schools is subject specific. Furthermore, although
the National Curriculum is not intended to represent the whole
of a pupil's curricular experiences, pressures of time will almost
inevitably result in priority being given to statutory programmes of study. Within the official documentation concerning these programmes of study, attention to the needs of pupils
with difficulties is primarily restricted to access for those with
physical or sensory impairments; for example, the phrase used
in both the geography and technology guidance: 'pupils unable
to communicate by speech, writing or drawing may use other
means including technology or symbols as alternatives'.

Throughout, there is little explicit consideration of the larger proportions of children with learning, emotional or behavioural difficulties.

However, a National Curriculum 'Task Group' on special educational needs has provided advice for schools on wider aspects of the implementation of the National Curriculum. In a preliminary circular (NCC 1989a) it takes up the point that schools themselves have a role to play in the difficulties experienced by their pupils, and asserts that those which: 'successfully meet the demands of a diverse range of individual needs through agreed policies on teaching and learning approaches are invariably effective in meeting special educational needs' (NCC 1989a: para. 5). Its subsequent guidance (NCC 1989b) highlights the importance of a whole school approach to curriculum planning, in which key themes are the need for co-operation both among staff and also with parents, colleagues in other schools and support agencies, and the need for flexibility.

The recognition that children's levels of attainments will be wide-ranging at any stage of their schooling certainly implies the need for flexibility in the delivery of the National Curriculum. This is particularly true for children with special educational needs who, by their very definition, experience significantly greater difficulties in learning than their peers, and whose attainments therefore may not always be well matched to the demands of the designated programmes of study for their Key Stage. Circular 6/89 (DES 1989a) suggests that, in certain circumstances, pupils may appropriately be taught at a level outside their Key Stage for part of the time, or, more controversially, that they may on occasion be grouped with peers of a different age. Some have argued that this second strategy is inconsistent with the principles of integration, and certainly the National Curriculum Council has expressed reservations about its desirability as well as its practicability. Whatever strategies are adopted, however, as Wedell (1990) has pointed out, it is not clear exactly how far flexible adaptations to the delivery of the curriculum can be taken before they become sufficiently significant that they should be regarded as formal modifications to the legal requirements.

The 1988 Act provides for two main ways in which the

National Curriculum may be formally 'modified' or even 'disapplied'. First, for individual pupils who have statements of special educational need, exceptions can be made to 'any or all' of the requirements of the National Curriculum. This will not automatically be necessary, but in those cases where exceptions are judged appropriate then the statements must be amended to indicate their precise nature, and must further specify the alternative provision that will be substituted in order to maintain a balanced and broadly based curriculum. Parents must be fully informed of any intended amendment to their child's statement, and have the right of appeal if they disagree with the LEA's decision. Second, temporary exceptions from the National Curriculum of up to six months, renewable for a further six months, may be sought. These may be specifically associated with a time when formal assessment procedures are being carried out which might lead to a statement of special educational need. A more general use is in situations where a pupil's 'circumstances' or 'conduct' are such as to make National Curriculum requirements inappropriate. The decision to seek a temporary exception rests largely with the headteacher, although he or she must inform the pupil's parents, as well as the school governors and the LEA, and the parents have a right of appeal. Not surprisingly, many concerns have been raised about the basis upon which judgements of the need for temporary exceptions might be made, and the DES has emphasized that they should be used only sparingly. The expectation, therefore, is that any formal exceptions from the National Curriculum will be minimal.

Most people would agree that this is consistent with the principles of the 1981 Act. Wedell (1990), for example, has argued that, although the programmes of study may require adaptation for some pupils, it would be hard to justify the 'disapplication' of any of the National Curriculum attainment targets 'in its entirety'. However, some of them may be of more apparent relevance to particular pupils than others, and the question of the relative weight given to different aspects of the curriculum is likely to require attention. Certainly the principle of entitlement to the National Curriculum, important though it undoubtedly is, should not lead to a denial of individual and specialized needs where they exist, and, as Norwich (1990) has indicated, the precise definition of what constitutes 'balance' in the curriculum may appropriately vary for different pupils.

On the whole, then, some concerns remain, both about the degree of flexibility with which the National Curriculum can be implemented, and also that the principle of entitlement should not become the sole basis upon which decisions about appropriate curricular activities are made. Nevertheless, many of the early reservations about the accessibility of the National Curriculum for children with special educational needs have been replaced by a cautious optimism.

Assessment procedures

The way in which progress through the National Curriculum is assessed is of particular significance for pupils who experience learning difficulties. Many who are concerned with special educational needs have welcomed the detailed teacher records which form an important part of the National Curriculum assessment process. The continuous curriculum-based assessment upon which such records should be based have a potentially valuable role to play not only in alerting teachers to areas of difficulty, but also in planning positive steps to overcome these and in monitoring progress.

The Standard Assessment Tasks, by contrast, have been greeted with far less enthusiasm, particularly where these involve the sort of 'paper and pencil' exercises which put many pupils with learning difficulties at a disadvantage. Formalized testing procedures are likely to be particularly stressful for those who lack confidence in themselves as learners, and unless they are sensitively undertaken they may contribute to feelings of failure. The Schools Examination and Assessment Council (SEAC 1989) has provided some reassurance that, in certain instances, minor adaptations can be made to the procedures; for example, in the length of time that is taken, the way in which instructions are given and the form of response that is required. This flexibility should, it believes, be sufficient to allow the vast majority of pupils with special educational needs to participate fully in the Standard Assessment Tasks. Questions may, of course, be raised about how far such adaptations can be taken and still yield 'standard' assessment information.

The main focus of concern, however, has been the use to which the results of Standard Assessment Tasks will be put. The publication of aggregated results is likely to become a significant means of comparing and judging school performance. As yet there is no central government acceptance of the argument that published results should be presented in a way that takes into account children's starting points, needs and progress. In the absence of this, and within the context of the 1988 Act's provisions on open enrolment and the local management of schools, many are apprehensive that the publication of aggregated results will work to the detriment of those with special educational needs.

Local management of schools

As a result of the Act, by far the largest part of an LEA's budget is devolved to its schools on a formula which is primarily based on the numbers and ages of pupils on roll. Coupled with the policy on open enrolment, this formula may effectively act to put schools in direct competition with one another in order to maintain their pupil numbers. Where that competition is based at least in part on the evidence of overall attainments on the National Curriculum, then the presence of a sizeable minority of pupils with learning difficulties will be disadvantageous to a school, and they may be perceived as an unwelcome and unproductive drain on resources. It has been argued that in such circumstances it is almost inevitable that the provision of teaching assistance for these pupils will be afforded a lower priority (Welton 1989). Furthermore, as their education is relatively expensive, schools may seek to restrict the numbers of children with special educational needs on their rolls unless they are seen to generate additional resourcing (Lunt 1990).

It is generally acknowledged that the introduction of local management of schools has made it harder for LEAs to safeguard such resourcing, particularly for those pupils without statements. There is scope for some weighting to be given in the formula by which funds are allocated to schools, but as the particular group of children concerned is so hard to define, accurate targeting of additional finance is problematic. The DES appears to recognize that there are grounds for concern, and has emphasized the need for LEAs and school governors 'to take steps to satisfy parents of children without statements that appropriate educational provision will be available to schools to meet their particular needs' (DES 1989b: para. 16). Unfortunately, however, as Upton (1990) has pointed out, it has not provided guidance about how this should be financed nor how LEAs can monitor the use made by schools of funds delegated for children with special educational needs. The situation is rather more straightforward for the pupils who have statements, where resources are allocated to them as individuals. There is, however, little doubt that the introduction of local management of schools has made more difficult the LEAs' task of planning coherent services for pupils with special educational needs.

These difficulties are likely to be compounded if increasing numbers of schools 'opt out' from their local authorities and become grant maintained, for inevitably this will leave fewer resources for support and advisory services and for the development of integration initiatives. Furthermore, it has been predicted that the schools most likely to choose grant-maintained status are those with the lowest percentages of pupils with special educational needs on their rolls. There is as yet insufficient evidence of 'opting out' to allow for an accurate assessment of how far this prediction is being met. If it proves to be so, however, it will result in proportionally fewer funds for distribution by LEAs to those schools most in need of additional assistance.

Summary

It can be seen that current concerns about the 1988 Act focus on its implications for the priority that can be given to special educational provision in the context of competitiveness between schools. It is precisely in the area of academic competition that those with special educational needs are most disadvantaged. There is already some evidence which could be taken to suggest that many schools are finding it more difficult to accommodate their needs since the Act was implemented. Thus, for example, recent surveys demonstrate that exclusion rates of pupils with emotional and behavioural difficulties have risen, and HMI has reported a significant increase in referrals for statements (Pyke 1991). These, taken together with a rise in the numbers of appeals against LEA decisions not to provide statements, may be indicative that problems in the resourcing of effective special educational provision in ordinary schools have been highlighted, if not exacerbated, by the implementation of the 1988 Act.

However, it is important to stress that, if we are to ensure that the rights of children with special educational needs are met, it is not simply a question of resourcing, but more fundamentally one of general attitudes and commitment. If the potential benefits of the 1988 Act are to be realized and its risks minimized, then this requires both positive attitudes and a determination to promote the educational opportunities of all pupils. The additional help that those with special educational needs require in order to overcome their learning difficulties is only likely to be safeguarded when they are afforded equal status and value to their peers. In such circumstances, it is possible to see how local financial management might enable schools to respond more rather than less flexibly to their needs. The National Curriculum has given pupils with special educational needs the right of access to a broader range of learning opportunities than they have often received in the past. As the National Curriculum Council (1989b) has emphasized, however, it is co-operation rather than competition which is necessary in order to help them derive the greatest possible benefit from this curricular entitlement.

Discussion points

1 How far should the education of children with special educational needs in ordinary schools be regarded as an equal opportunities issue? Consider the role of staff attitudes and commitment in developing a positive whole school approach to special educational provision.

2 Children with special educational needs are almost inevitably disadvantaged in an ethos of academic competitiveness. Yet it can be argued that an emphasis on non-academic aspects of their achievements leads to lowered expectations and restricted educational opportunities. With these points in mind, consider how far the provisions of the 1988 Act are compatible with the aims and principles of the 1981 Act.

3 Statements – an important safeguard of resources for those with the greatest needs, or an unnecessary way of categorizing children? What do you see as the main advantages and limitations of the statementing process?

Further reading

Daniels, H. and Ware, J. (eds) (1990) *Special Educational Needs and the National Curriculum*, Bedford Way Series, London: Kogan Page.

Welton, J., Wedell, K. and Vorhaus, G. (1982) *Meeting Special Educational Needs: The 1981 Act and Its Implications*, Bedford Way Paper No. 12, London: Heinemann.

Note

Since this chapter was written, the Government has published a new Education Bill (1992) which incorporates much of the 1981 Act. A number of modifications to the provisions of the 1981 Act are proposed, including the setting up of a Special Educational Needs Tribunal, and it is possible that further changes may be introduced as the Bill passes through parliament.

3 The range of special educational need and provision

Special educational need arises from a complex interaction of personal and environmental factors, and may be viewed as a mismatch between the emotional, social and learning demands that are made of a pupil and the resources that the pupil has to meet these demands. It follows, therefore, that the difficulties a pupil experiences cannot be seen in isolation from the context in which they occur. In the majority of cases, special educational need will be identified at school, when aspects of a pupil's progress or behaviour give cause for concern. Because educational needs are relative to the learning contexts that pupils experience, and to the attitudes and expectations of others, teacher judgements about pupils are likely to be affected by the general levels of attainment in a class, as well as by school and LEA practice. Further, it seems clear that gender, home background, socio-economic and ethnic variables are also often associated with the process of identification of special educational need. Thus, while within-child factors may play an important part in learning or behavioural difficulties, these should not be seen in isolation from the contribution of home, school and wider social influences.

Nevertheless, for a minority of pupils the assessment of special educational need will be based primarily on the diagnosis of some specific impairment which restricts their ability to participate fully in the educational opportunities that are generally available. It is important, therefore, that teachers are aware of the nature of such impairments. Usually, although not always, these are likely to have been detected prior to a child starting school. More boys than girls may be affected, but, unlike the larger categories of special educational need, the presence of specific impairment is not associated with particular socio-economic variables.

Specific forms of impairment

It is important to emphasize that the relationship between a particular impairment and a child's educational needs is not a straightforward one. Any significant impairment gives rise to certain disabilities or limitations, but the extent to which these 'handicap' the child will depend on his or her strengths as well as weaknesses, and will also reflect the degree of support and understanding that is provided at home, at school and in the community more generally. As a result, a wide range of variation can be described in both the needs and educational progress that are experienced by children who have similar levels of impairment. It is clear, however, that close co-operation and liaison between home, school and other involved professionals is vital if their needs are to be most effectively met. In the following discussion, attention is drawn to some of the main forms of impairment that teachers may meet in ordinary schools, but it should be stressed that this does not represent a comprehensive overview. Further, although these have been categorized as sensory, physical and cognitive, it is important to note that there may often be an overlap between these impairments, and it is not always easy to distinguish which is the more significant in terms of its educational implications.

Sensory impairments

Complete loss of either hearing or vision is rare, but any significant degree of impairment involving these senses restricts the means by which children are able to integrate their experiences and make sense of their environments. As a result, they may find their learning contexts less predictable and secure than they appear to others. There is, of course, likely to be variation in acuity of hearing and vision within any class, and some of the management implications that result from the presence of pupils with diagnosed sensory impairments, such as attention to lighting, noise level, physical organization and flexible modes of instruction, may well benefit others in the group.

It is estimated that about one in a thousand children have a severe hearing loss, and almost two more in each thousand have a loss which requires the use of an aid (Bishop and Gregory 1986). Less severe and intermittent losses, which are far more frequent, may play a significant part in many children's educational difficulties. Hearing impairment can be described as 'sensorineural' or 'conductive'. The first term refers to a loss resulting from damage to the inner ear or auditory nerve and associated brain cells. This is usually irreversible, and in about half of all cases it is thought to be attributable to genetic factors. Other causes can include maternal contraction of German measles in the early months of pregnancy, as well as childhood viral infections such as meningitis. By contrast, conductive hearing losses result from some blockage or damage to the outer or middle ear, and these are usually both less severe and also more likely to be treatable. The most common cause is the middle ear infection often referred to as 'glue ear', which occurs and can recur during childhood. This leads to fluctuating levels of hearing which, if not detected, are likely to affect both language acquisition and general progress at school. It is not uncommon to find that children have been labelled as 'unco-operative', 'lazy' or 'inattentive' because of unnoticed hearing losses and it is, therefore, very important that teachers are alert to any signs that a pupil may not be hearing adequately. It cannot be assumed that the child will draw explicit attention to the difficulties that arise as, particularly in the early years of schooling, children may not be able to monitor such changes in their hearing acuity for themselves.

The majority of children with hearing impairment are educated in ordinary schools, where, particularly in cases of severe loss, they and their teachers should receive some support from specialist peripatetic teachers. The nature of that support will vary according to individual needs, but is likely to include guidance on how to maximize the use of the hearing that a child does have, as well as on the development of appropriate communication strategies. Whether or not children require hearing aids, the acoustics of the room, the level of background noise, their positioning for full class and group activities, and the clarity with which their teachers communicate will all affect how successfully they can use their hearing. A number of different forms of aid may be used which act to amplify those sounds that the child is capable of hearing. Conventional aids pick up all the sounds within a limited range, and amplify most of those that are nearest to the wearer. By contrast, radio-microphone aids allow for the selective amplification of the voice of a teacher who is wearing a microphone, and operate over a much greater distance. In some cases, a 'loop' system may be installed round the perimeter of a room which enables a better quality of sound to be received by those wearing aids.

There has been a long-standing debate about which means of communication should be the primary focus in teaching children with severe hearing impairments. Some favour oral methods which emphasize the medium of the spoken word, whereas others advocate the use of signing. British Sign Language is the natural language of the deaf community in Britain, and in recent years it has increasingly been argued that it should be regarded as a first language by those teaching deaf children. A further approach, known as Total Communication, which has also gained in popularity, seeks to combine speech and signing together with other non-verbal aspects of communication.

The major educational disadvantage for children with hearing impairment derives from limitations in their language experiences. The potential effects of unresolved difficulties in this area are wide-ranging, involving personal, social and cognitive aspects of their learning at school (Webster and Wood 1989). A fundamental need for children with such impairments, therefore, is for the fullest possible opportunities to develop their communication skills, using whatever residual hearing and other means that are available to help them.

Unlike hearing impairment, significant visual impairment is comparatively rare among children of school age. Its cause is not always known but it may either be present from birth or be acquired subsequently. Assessment of the extent of impairment is based on measured acuity after correction with lenses, and also takes account of any restriction in the field of vision. Children who are partially sighted can, with help, use print in their learning and thus their educational needs are primarily concerned with the use of aids and materials to assist this means of access to the school curriculum. Those who are assessed as blind will usually have some light reception and may have further residual sight which can be used, but they are unable to read print of any size. They therefore require alternatives, such as Braille, tactile diagrams and 'talking books' (recorded on to audiotape), if they are to participate fully in the curriculum. They are also likely to need special help in order to develop their orientation and independent mobility in the environment. There has been a considerable increase in the integration of visually impaired pupils, although practice varies from LEA to LEA (Dawkins 1991). Where partially sighted and blind children are educated in ordinary schools, they and their teachers should be supported by specialist teachers of the visually impaired. These staff can provide guidance on lighting, materials and the use of specific aids in the classroom. They may also work individually with pupils, for example, to develop their skills in Braille. Where such specialist input is necessary, it is important that there is close liaison and joint planning with class teachers in order to ensure that it is incorporated as far as possible into the pupil's broader experiences of the curriculum.

The loss of vision has implications for a number of aspects of learning. For example, communication may be hampered where children have difficulty in picking up non-verbal cues, and active interaction with the environment may also be inhibited. Furthermore, reading, whether by Braille or from magnified print, is a laborious and lengthy process. It is important, therefore, that teachers give attention to the timing of tasks which require such reading, and that they also draw on a variety of alternative media, both auditory and tactile, to support the pupils' learning (Chapman and Stone 1988). Where vision is the only area of impairment, with appropriate help and support children are generally reported to achieve levels of attainment similar to those of their sighted peers, although they may need longer in order to do so.

Physical impairment

Explicit attention to the educational needs that are associated with poorly developed motor co-ordination will be necessary in any classroom group. Henderson and Sugden (1991), for example, estimate that up to 15 per cent of pupils have a degree of physical impairment which can interfere with their progress at school. Among these will be a large number of pupils who appear physically 'normal', but who have considerable difficulty in tasks which involve motor co-ordination. Often referred to as 'clumsy', they can experience difficulties not only in their learning but also in their self-confidence and social relationships if their needs are not recognized.

Where pupils have a more specific physical impairment their ability to interact with the environment will be limited in some way. However, because of the diversity of such impairments, it is difficult to generalize about the nature of the special needs that are likely to arise. On the whole, if their impairment is limited to particular muscles or limbs, then children's needs are primarily likely to be for therapy and care, together with special means of access to the curriculum. By contrast, where there is neurological damage, as for example in cerebral palsy and spina bifida, this can lead to additional sensory and learning difficulties.

The term cerebral palsy refers to a group of movement disorders resulting from damage to the developing brain. This damage is usually associated with trauma at around the time of birth, such as a lack of oxygen to the brain, although less often damage may occur later. The most common forms of cerebral palsy are spasticity, characterized by stiff movements of the affected limbs, and athetosis, which results in writhing or jerky involuntary movements. The extent and severity of the motor impairment vary widely, as does the degree of any additional difficulty. Vision, hearing and speech articulation can be affected, and there is an increased likelihood of epilepsy. Intellectual functioning may also be impaired, although this is not necessarily the case, and the educational attainments of some children with cerebral palsy are at least as high as those of their able-bodied contemporaries.

Spina bifida is a condition in which damage occurs to the spinal cord during pregnancy. The resulting physical difficulties range from mild to severe. This depends on the location and extent of the damage, for it affects the child's control of his or her body below that point. As a result, children with spina bifida can often have limited or no use of their lower limbs and may be incontinent. Many also have hydrocephalus, a build-up of cerebro-spinal fluid in the ventricles of the brain, which if unchecked can lead to further damage, but which is usually controlled by the insertion of a valve or 'shunt' to drain the fluid into the bloodstream. As with cerebral palsy, the full range of cognitive competence is found among children affected by spina bifida, although it has been suggested that those with hydro-cephalus often have additional learning difficulties (Henderson and Sugden 1991).

It can be seen then that different forms of physical impairment may lead to a variety of individual needs. Special physical and health needs, such as for physiotherapy or help with mobility and continence, require liaison and co-ordination between teachers and other professionals. One area for consideration here is likely to be the balance between time spent in meeting such needs and that which is necessary to ensure that a pupil has the opportunity to participate in the full range of general curricular activities. Modification of task materials and the use of special aids or equipment may be required to help pupils engage with these activities, and more time may be needed to allow for the completion of tasks. Attention to the physical layout of the classroom will also be required, for this will need to be designed to maximize ease of movement and access to resources. At the same time, though, the presence of additional aids and equipment will have implications for the way in which available space can be most effectively managed. Furthermore, adaptations may be necessary throughout a school, for example to doors and stairways, in order to facilitate mobility and access for pupils with physical impairments.

Cognitive and other impairments

By comparison with the sorts of impairment so far discussed, the identification of causes of cognitive limitations is far less straightforward. In some cases, just as with sensory and physical impairment, it is clear that cognitive impairment can be associated with genetic factors and maternal conditions during pregnancy such as infections, diet and drug use, as well as with birth complications and subsequent childhood illness and injury. However, it is also evident that environmental influences play a significant part, and that the interaction of within-child and environmental factors is complex. As a result, early developmental delays and difficulties may often prove to be temporary, and even where they persist it is frequently not possible to identify a specific cause.

Among the minority of children with persistent and generalized delays in their development for whom specific causes have been identified, those with Down's syndrome stand out as the largest single group. This syndrome results from a chromosomal abnormality, usually in the form of an extra chromosome 21, and it is frequently associated with additional difficulties, among which the most common are heart defects and hearing loss. Although those with the syndrome share a number of distinctive physical characteristics, there is far wider diversity in their development than is sometimes appreciated. In the past, a diagnosis of Down's syndrome was very often taken to imply 'severe subnormality' (and thus, prior to 1970, 'ineducability'), but there has been an increasing recognition of individual variation in the nature and extent of their educational needs. That is, while some children do experience severe learning difficulties, the difficulties of others have been assessed as moderate or mild. As a result, more children with Down's syndrome are being educated in ordinary schools and individual educational attainments at GCSE level have recently been reported. Early educational intervention may do much to promote their development and learning (Cunningham 1988), and with appropriate help some children with Down's syndrome have acquired reading skills prior to starting school (Buckley 1985). Overall, it seems evident that there is much still to be learned about the full range of educational outcomes which may be achieved. The cognitive difficulties of children with Down's syndrome are generally reported to lie primarily in consolidating and generalizing their skills, and where this is so they require carefully planned and structured activities to facilitate their learning.

Very much rarer, but included here because the term has become a familiar one, is the diagnosis of autism. Although the precise causes of this severe and complex syndrome are still unclear, research evidence points to an impairment of cognitive functioning (Frith 1989). Children with autism are typically described as having difficulties in communication skills and social relationships, and as showing inflexibility in aspects of their behaviour which may become ritualized into fixed routines. Their speech can be echolalic (repeating what has been heard), and the use of eye contact, gestural or facial expression as well as the timing of conversational turn-taking may all be affected. They often demonstrate a rather limited awareness of the intentions or moods of others and appear to have difficulty in making sense of their social environment. There is a wide range of variation among children with autism, and some may demonstrate exceptional skills in a specific area of development, such as in music, art or mathematical calculation. In most cases though they have significant and often severe learning difficulties, and, although some have been placed in ordinary classes with support, the majority are taught in special schools or units.

Cognitive and language development are interrelated in important ways, and therefore it is not surprising to find that children with cognitive impairments also typically show delays, and in some cases disorders, in their language acquisition. As previously discussed, such difficulties can also result from sensory impairments and, indeed, temporary language delays are not rare during the early years of childhood. Infrequently, however, specific and longer lasting problems occur, not only in articulation but also involving impairments in the interpretation of the sounds and grammar of speech or in the communicative functions of language. Where these difficulties are particularly severe, pupils tend to receive at least part of their education in separate provision. However, when it is felt that a pupil would benefit more from being taught with peers who are competent language users, then they may be placed in an ordinary school context. In such cases, with support from speech therapists and/or specialist language teachers, additional help and guidance will focus primarily on appropriate classroom communication strategies (Webster and McConnell 1987).

Some children with language impairments may also have problems in acquiring literacy skills. The identification of such problems is, of course, usually made at school. Reading difficulty is particularly prevalent among pupils with special educational needs, and this is a reflection both of the importance attached to literacy and also, as discussed later in this chapter, of the way in which educational progress is assessed. In many cases poor progress in reading may be symptomatic of general difficulties in learning, but in others it may provide evidence of a more specific educational need. That is, some children experience significant difficulties in their reading but not in other unrelated areas of their learning. Specific reading difficulty is often referred to as dyslexia, although it is important to note that some controversy surrounds the use of the term. Definitions of what constitutes specific reading difficulty vary, and so, accordingly do estimates of its incidence. The Dyslexia Institute suggests that as many as one in twenty-five children may be affected. It characterizes dyslexia as a distinctive pattern of learning difficulties that is particularly associated with the acquisition of phonological reading strategies. Others question whether these difficulties represent a specific 'condition' which gives rise to needs that are qualitatively different from those experienced by the larger number of children whose reading skills are delayed (e.g. Tyre and Young 1991). What is not in doubt, however, is that there is a minority of pupils whose reading attainments are significantly below the standards they achieve in other areas of learning, and who, like others with more general difficulties, require help and support both to build on their strengths and to meet their particular needs.

Throughout this discussion of some of the forms of impairment that can contribute to special educational need it has been emphasized that there is considerable variation in the impact these may have on individual children. This variation will in part be determined by the severity and extent of impairment, but also by the quality of the learning experiences that are provided. Where the nature and extent of the child's difficulties are such that additional or special help will be required at school, then following formal assessment procedures a statement of special educational need should be provided by the LEA.

The wider range of special educational need

It must be re-emphasized that the identification of special educational need is only associated with a diagnosis of specific impairment in a small percentage of cases. For most pupils with special educational needs, the difficulties that arise at school cannot be attributed to a particular impairment. Rather, these difficulties will involve some less easily defined lack of match between the pupils' personal resources and the demands that are made of them. Accordingly, the identification of special educational needs is primarily based on teacher judgement that a pupil's levels of attainment and/or behaviour are significantly poorer than those of the pupil's peers.

Prior to the introduction of the National Curriculum, most LEAS employed routine screening procedures of all pupils in their schools at particular ages, typically in the form of reading tests (Gipps, Gross and Goldstein 1987). The use made of the results of these tests varied from authority to authority, but children whose scores relative to their age fell below a particular cut-off point might be identified as in need of further assessment. In practice, any authority-wide procedures tend to operate as a safety net, because most LEAs have written guidelines which make it clear that it is the responsibility of individual schools to identify and make provision for the special educational needs of their pupils (Goacher et al. 1988).

The apparent incidence and nature of special educational need, as Croll and Moses (1985) have pointed out, is therefore fundamentally associated with the formal and informal assessment procedures that are used by teachers in school. While there is considerable variation between schools in their assessment and monitoring systems, their records of pupils' progress are likely to incorporate both teacher observation and also more standardized tests or curriculum-based checklists. In the junior schools studied by Croll and Moses the predominant type of standardized assessment was some form of reading test: by far the largest category of special educational need identified by the teachers was learning difficulty (over 15 per cent of all pupils), and this was almost always characterized as involving problems in reading. The test scores of most of the children who were described as having such difficulties were at least twelve months below their chronological age, and for a minority they represented a delay in attainment of twenty-four months or more. However, it was not only the test scores which appeared to influence the teachers' judgements, as the identification of difficulty was also associated with the general reading standards in the class and with particular pupil characteristics. Thus younger children, boys and those whose behaviour was judged problematic were all more likely to be identified as having reading difficulties. Nearly all the pupils with reading difficulties were also regarded by their teachers as 'slow learners', but there were few references to other specific aspects of learning difficulty, such as in mathematics or problem-solving.

It would appear then that both at LEA and at school level, at least during the primary years, assessment of reading attainment is central to the identification of special educational need. This is not surprising, for reading is a skill which is highly valued by parents, schools and society, and furthermore it is a major means of access to many other aspects of the curriculum. However, too often poor reading skills can lead to lowered expectations of a pupil's achievements in other areas of learning. For some pupils, their difficulties may be specific to reading, or, less frequently identified by schools, to other skill areas. Even where they experience generalized difficulties in their learning the label of 'slow learner' is both imprecise and unhelpful, for there will be individual variation in pace of learning in any classroom, and all pupils are likely to demonstrate areas of relative strength and weakness across the curriculum.

It may be that the implementation of the National

Curriculum assessment procedures will encourage a fuller profile of pupils' attainments, at least in certain subject areas. If
used positively this could both serve to boost pupils' confidence
in themselves as learners, by drawing attention to particular
strengths, and also pinpoint areas of weakness which require
additional help. By contrast, if difficulties in one aspect of
learning lead to generalized expectations of low achievement
across the curriculum, then a pupil's experiences of school are
likely to be increasingly unrewarding. Successful learning makes
considerable demands on children's personal resources. Anxiety
or expectation of failure may often lead to a loss of motivation
and self-esteem which can only compound the experience of
learning difficulty, and it is therefore unsurprising that poor
educational attainment is frequently associated with emotional
or behavioural difficulties. It is important to note, however, that
such an association is not inevitable. It is less probable in
situations where children feel supported and encouraged in their
learning, are provided with real opportunities for success and,
importantly, can see that their achievements are both
recognized and valued.

Emotional and behavioural difficulties form the second
largest category of special educational need identified in school,
although it is unusual to find that this is the only type of
difficulty a pupil experiences. The nature and extent of
emotional and behavioural problems are wide-ranging and,
apart from in the most severe cases, difficult to define. Teacher
judgements are based on their professional experience and are
likely to incorporate comparisons with the general standard of
conduct in the class. Inevitably though, they may also be
influenced by personal values and expectations about 'appropriate' social and emotional behaviour. Typically, boys are more
likely than girls to be identified as having emotional and
behavioural difficulties, as are pupils from particular minority
ethnic backgrounds (Tomlinson 1982).

Any assessment of difficulty must take into account the
interactive context in which it arises and, because teachers are so
involved with that context, it can be difficult for them to analyse
those aspects that may be contributing factors. It has been
suggested (e.g. ILEA 1985) that teachers are less alert to signs of

emotional difficulty that create problems for the individual pupil than they are to the more overt behaviour that presents them with problems of class control. Others, however (e.g. Croll and Moses 1985), argue that teachers do differentiate between problems of discipline and other forms of emotional and behavioural difficulty. On the whole, it would seem that pupils are identified by their teachers where their behaviour is judged to interfere with their own learning or that of other pupils, or to disrupt their relationships with peers and staff. Their needs are particularly associated with the social and emotional climate for learning as they experience it. They are fundamentally associated, therefore, with the quality of the relationships that the pupils are helped to develop in school. There is, therefore, a consensus of opinion that teachers can do much to alleviate their difficulties by adopting effective classroom management strategies which promote high levels of involvement in successful learning opportunities. These strategies are discussed in Chapter 6.

The identification of special educational need is not an end in itself, but should be the starting point for action to help pupils overcome their difficulties. The Warnock Committee envisaged a phased process of assessment and intervention which began with the class teacher but might subsequently involve increasing numbers of professionals, and which for a minority of pupils would culminate in the provision of a statement of special educational need. Policies for the school-based stages of this assessment vary between LEAs, but in the majority of cases it is only when planned and recorded interventions within school have failed to help meet a child's needs that the school is likely to initiate the formal procedures that may result in the drawing up of a statement.

Thus, an example of the school-based stages of assessment might be as follows:

(i)   A teacher who identifies concerns about a particular pupil will make an observational assessment of the nature of the difficulties that are being experienced. A comparison of the pupil's responses to different learning activities and teaching approaches should enable the teacher to identify possible class-based strategies which might be effective.

(ii) If difficulties persist, the teacher's records form the basis for consultation and discussion with the special needs co-ordinator and headteacher, about the next appropriate steps to be taken. There is some evidence that the possible contribution of sensory, physical and health factors to difficulties in learning or behaviour can be underestimated by teachers, and it is therefore important that the accuracy of the available information from school records is checked. Advice should be sought from the pupil's parents and, wherever possible, both they and the pupil should be fully involved in the decision-making process. It is likely that further observational assessments will need to be undertaken in school, perhaps involving both class teachers and the special needs co-ordinator. These will inform the planning of more specific intervention, the effectiveness of which will be closely monitored.

(iii) If the steps taken have not helped the pupil overcome the difficulties, it might be decided that further assessment advice is required, for example, from an educational psychologist, therapist or specialist advisory teacher. Depending on the nature of this advice, the school is often able to draw upon its existing resources and available levels of support in order to provide the special assistance that the pupil is judged to need.

(iv) Where this is not possible, however, it is at this stage that the school will refer the pupil to the LEA for multi-professional assessment in order to determine whether a statement is required.

The range of special educational provision

Whether or not pupils have statements of special educational need, a generally accepted principle in determining appropriate provision is that, wherever possible, identified needs should be met without any unnecessary separation from their peers. The majority are, and have always been, educated in ordinary schools and on the whole, the better the level and quality of provision that is available in regular classes, the more likely it is that most needs can be met there. Some would argue (e.g. Galloway 1985, Dessent 1987) that if an effective 'whole school approach' to special educational provision is developed then there is little justification for the separation of pupils into special groups, units or classes. Others, however (e.g. Norwich 1990), point out that such organizational arrangements can be beneficial to particular pupils, and are only likely to have negative consequences if they provide educational opportunities that are of lower quality and status than those available in ordinary classes.

The Warnock Committee identified four main types of special educational provision that might be made in ordinary schools:

(i) 'Full-time education in an ordinary class with any necessary help or support';
(ii) 'education in an ordinary class with periods of withdrawal to a special class or unit or other supporting base';
(iii) 'education in a special class or unit with periods of attendance at an ordinary class and full involvement in the general community life and extra-curricular activities of the ordinary school';
(iv) 'full-time education in a special class or unit with social contact with the main school'.

(DES 1978: para. 7.12)

In some respects these may be seen to form a continuum from ordinary to more specialized educational provision and can be extended further, first to those special schools that have a variety of educational and social links with their neighbourhood schools, and finally to the small number that operate quite separately. Variations on this continuum of provision exist in most authorities. However, although most pupils in special schools have statements and most in ordinary schools do not, it is not possible to draw simple parallels between a continuum of needs and one of provision. In some authorities, statements are rarely maintained if pupils transfer from special to ordinary schools and, conversely, the issuing of a statement for a pupil who has begun his or her education in ordinary school may typically result in a move to a special school. By contrast, other authorities seek to educate children with statements in ordinary schools wherever possible. The decisions that are made about the most appropriate provision for those with special educational needs are clearly influenced by the resources that are available. They are also fundamentally affected by the attitudes towards integration that are held by LEAs, teachers, parents and, less frequently taken into account, the pupils themselves.

Attitudes to integrated educational provision

In order to explore attitudes towards integrated educational provision, it is necessary first to consider the range of different meanings that can be associated with the term 'integration'. The Warnock Committee distinguished between three main forms of integration: 'locational' integration occurs when special units or classes are attached to, or share a site with, ordinary schools; 'social' integration refers to situations where the unit's pupils 'eat, play and consort with other children, and possibly share organised out-of-classroom activities'; and 'functional' or the fullest form of integration is achieved if, in addition to social contacts, those with special educational needs join the regular school classes on a full- or part-time basis.

This was, as the Committee acknowledged, a rather basic model, and it has resulted in some over-simplified interpretations of what integrated provision involves. First, it has led to a greater emphasis on placement than on the quality of the pupil's educational experiences. Fish (ILEA 1985) has argued that integration should be conceptualized as a process rather than a state, and one which implies 'continued and planned interaction with contemporaries'. Although it is clear that this requires at least intermittent physical proximity, the placement of children together in the same classroom, dining area or school grounds is not in itself sufficient to promote social or functional integration. As Hegarty and his colleagues (1981) have pointed out, a pupil who usually works with an assistant in an ordinary classroom may be as segregated from other pupils as one who is withdrawn for special support. Similarly, a pupil who is educated in a separate unit in the school may experience fewer opportunities for integration than one who visits from a special school for regular joint activities.

Equally important has been the criticism that integration has become narrowly defined to concern only those children who have traditionally been educated in segregated provision. From this perspective, 'Integration is *their* problem, and success is when they are assimilated into an ordinary school' (Hegarty *et al*. 1981: 15). Such a view may underlie the approach to integration that Jones (1983) has described as a 'limpet' model, in which children are attached as a separate group to a school 'in the hope that some waves of normality will wash over them'. Even where more functional integration is aimed for, too often an attempt may be made to fit the children into a system which was not designed with their needs in mind. By contrast, where integration is regarded as having relevance to all pupils, both those with special educational needs and also their peers, then the emphasis is more appropriately placed on the changes that might be necessary in the school as a whole in order to respond to the full range of their needs.

There are, then, rather differing interpretations of what is implied by the term integration, and these will inevitably affect attitudes towards integrated educational provision. Concerns about the availability of specialist skills and knowledge in ordinary schools may lead some parents of children with statements to express a preference for separate provision (Sandow *et al*. 1987), and among special school pupils there seems to be no clear-cut consensus of opinion about the relative advantages and disadvantages of separate and integrated education (ILEA 1985). Among both parents and their children, the opportunity for access to wider curricular experiences in ordinary schools may often be welcomed, but reservations are commonly expressed about the level of support and understanding they may receive there from both teachers and other pupils. It is clear that their views are likely to be strongly influenced by the quality of their experience of integrated or separate provision, and the same is undoubtedly true for teachers.

Teachers' attitudes are likely to be influenced by their feelings of confidence about their professional competence to meet special educational needs and by the availability of appropriate support to help them in this task. Where their perspectives have been sought on the functional integration of special school pupils, they are generally reported to be far more positive about those with physical or sensory impairments than those with moderate learning difficulties or emotional and behavioural difficulties. As Croll and Moses (1985) have pointed out, often teachers may not be fully aware of the educational implications associated with particular physical and sensory impairments, but they are all likely to have had direct experience of the teaching and management challenges that can be posed by significant difficulties in learning and behaviour. These are, however, not only the most frequently occurring forms of special educational need, but also the most complex to define. Factors such as gender, race and home background have all been seen to be involved in the distinctions that are drawn between the level of difficulty that might be met in regular classrooms and that which requires additional or specialist help. It is possible, therefore, that as awareness of the interactive and relative nature of their needs is heightened in ordinary schools, more positive attitudes will develop towards the integration of pupils with such difficulties.

There is some evidence to support the view that increased knowledge and understanding of special educational needs may lead to different perspectives. For example, a study of the attitudes of teachers who had been trained as special needs co-ordinators (Sugden *et al.* 1989) found that, provided in-service opportunities were made for school staff, the vast majority were in favour of integrated provision for pupils with moderate learning difficulties. Further, with additional staffing resources, they also supported the education of those with emotional and behavioural difficulties in ordinary schools. By contrast, most of the co-ordinators felt that the integration of pupils with sensory or physical impairments was only appropriate if they were supported by specialist teachers.

Thus it would appear that, with increasing awareness and acceptance of the role of ordinary schools in making special educational provision, attitudes towards integration may begin to shift. The main forms of special educational need identified by the Warnock Committee (DES 1978) were for means of access to the curriculum, worthwhile and successful learning experiences and a supportive educational environment. These needs will be present for a significant minority of pupils in any school. On the whole, it seems reasonable to suppose that those schools that are most successful in meeting existing needs will also respond most positively to the further integration of pupils with more specialized needs.

Discussion points

1 In 1981, Hegarty and his colleagues referred to a prevalent view that integration was '*their* problem', that is, the problem of children with special educational needs. To what extent. should integration be seen as problematic, and for whom?
2 'Disabilities and difficulties become more or less handi-capping depending on the expectations of others and on social contexts' (ILEA 1985). How far would you agree with this proposition? Consider what strategies might be available to teachers in order to ensure that pupils with disabilities are not unnecessarily 'handicapped' in school.
3 The vast majority of special educational needs are identified at school when pupils fail in some way to meet the demands that are made of them. Discuss the role of teacher attitudes and expectations in the identification of learning and emotional or behavioural difficulties.

Further reading

Dessent, T. (1987) *Making the Ordinary School Special*, Lewes: Falmer.
National Children's Bureau (1991) *Signposts to Special Needs*, Nottingham: NES Arnold.

4 A curriculum for all?

The implementation of the National Curriculum gave, for the first time, a legal entitlement to all children to share in a set of common curricular experiences. This requires that school staff are committed to the provision of a curriculum that is 'broad, balanced, relevant and differentiated' (NCC 1989b), and will meet the full range of pupils' needs.

In order to explore the way in which this provision might be developed, it is helpful to consider the approaches to the curriculum that have influenced special education in the past. Special schools have generally been free from some of the constraints, such as external examinations, that apply in mainstream education and, perhaps as a result, there are many examples of innovative practice in their curriculum development (Mittler and Farrell 1987). However, the focus has tended to be more on the special than on the common educational needs of their pupils, and the curriculum has often been quite separate from that found in ordinary schools (Gulliford 1985). A particular strength has been in the explicit attention that has been paid to aspects of learning that tend to remain part of the 'hidden' curriculum in mainstream education. Thus, there is usually an emphasis on planned activities which aim to enhance both feelings of personal worth and also confidence and competence in social interaction. By contrast, a risk associated with specially designed provision is that it may lead to an underestimation of the pupils. Such a risk is heightened if the curriculum is narrowly focused and allows little access to mainstream learning experiences. Indeed, the most frequently voiced criticism of special school provision in the past has concerned the lack of curricular breadth.

Within ordinary schools, pupils with special educational needs can have access to a wider range of educational opportunities than their special school peers, but there is little evidence to suggest that the curriculum has often been designed with their needs in mind. Consequently, they have frequently followed a more restricted curriculum than others in the school, typically with a particular emphasis on basic literacy and numeracy skills. In the past, at secondary school, for example, those with learning difficulties have tended to have limited access to specialist subject teachers, and have often followed separate syllabuses and specially designed option courses (Clunies-Ross and Wimhurst 1983). More recently, some schools have adopted a 'whole school' approach to special educational provision. The exact form that this takes varies from school to school, but an example from one school is shown in Figure 4.1. As this illustrates, a key principle is that all staff retain responsibility for the education of all pupils.

With increasing moves towards a whole school approach, it may be the case that pupils are less frequently taught in separate groups or classes. Further, the implementation of the National Curriculum should result in their access to a wider range of educational experiences than might previously have been the case. However, as HMI surveys (1989, 1991) have demonstrated, curricular breadth is not enough by itself to ensure that pupils are provided with 'balanced' and 'differentiated' learning experiences. It is, therefore, important to explore what these terms might imply for those with special educational needs.

The Warnock Committee saw the aims of education as twofold:

> first, to enlarge a child's knowledge, experience and imaginative understanding, and thus his awareness of moral values and capacity for enjoyment; and secondly, to enable him to enter the world after formal education is over as an active participant in society and a responsible contributor to it, capable of achieving as much independence as possible.
>
> (DES, 1978: para. 1.4)

The question of 'balance' between the individual and social aims of education identified here can be seen as central to curriculum

This framework [for a whole school approach] . . . assumes that the school AS A WHOLE recognizes the needs of all its pupils and this particularly includes those who may have special educational needs. The whole school is involved in the education and development of these pupils.

It assumes that each pupil will have access to:

(a) an appropriate curriculum;
(b) specialist help if this is required;
(c) an appropriate social and emotional climate;
(d) counselling and support.

Providing access to an appropriate curriculum is of paramount importance and is the measure by which we could judge our success in providing fully for the educational needs of all our pupils.

Developing positive attitudes towards pupils' needs and their rights to an appropriate education are fundamental if the school is going to develop a truly whole school approach. Similarly, it has to be accepted that the expertise of many people will be needed if pupils' needs are to be met and if appropriate curricula are to be presented.

The basic premise on which we should be working is that no one person should be seen as being responsible for the assessment of needs and neither should one person be responsible for meeting needs. To assess and meet the needs of our pupils demands a co-ordinated team effort in which each member of the team clearly understands his or her role. It follows on from this that clear role definitions are essential as are clear and well defined lines of communication.

Figure 4.1 Extracts from a secondary school's discussion paper on 'A Whole School Approach to Special Educational Needs'

development for all pupils. It becomes a critical consideration for pupils with special educational needs, because for them it also concerns the relative weighting that should appropriately be given to common and more specialized educational aims. Accordingly it has considerable implications for the time that is made available for sharing the curricular experiences of their peers.

It is important to emphasize that entitlement to a common curriculum does not imply that identical learning activities and teaching approaches will be relevant to the needs of all children. The notion of 'differentiation' refers to the way in which these might be flexibly matched to pupils' experience, skills,

same objective but
differentiated

knowledge and interests. Alternative models of curriculum development in special education have been concerned with both balance and differentiation. The approaches that have been followed, however, have been influenced not only by the nature of particular needs, but also by the way in which these have been conceptualized.

Early approaches to curriculum development in special education

Early approaches to curriculum development were influenced by the view that special educational needs arose primarily from within-child factors. Where children were regarded as simply 'slow', a 'watered down' and somewhat impoverished version of the mainstream curriculum would generally have been considered appropriate. Alternatively, when special educational needs were deemed evidence of some specific deficit, there was a view that it might be possible to identify and somehow restore 'the missing skills which . . . [would] enable them to join the mainstream curriculum again' (Swann 1988b). Thus, for example, it might be the case that pupils were found to have difficulties in tasks which involved auditory or visual discrimination. Where this was so, it was assumed that specific training in these skills would enhance their learning throughout the curriculum. Accordingly, structured programmes were developed whereby pupils were taught to recognize and discriminate between visual or auditory patterns of increasing complexity. The programmes frequently led to improved pupil performance on the set tasks. Not surprisingly, however, when these skills were taught in isolation they were rarely found to transfer to other areas of learning. Increasingly, therefore, doubts were raised about the validity of trying to isolate and 'treat' apparent problems in this way. As a result, the effectiveness of the approach, as well as its relevance to the curriculum as a whole, was brought into question.

This is not to suggest that methods that focus on perceived within-child deficits no longer exist. For example, in the minority of cases where pupils have specific impairments which impede their learning, it may well be thought appropriate to

incorporate special aims into their general curricular experiences. Nevertheless, by the late 1970s, dissatisfaction had
grown with what could generally be achieved by a curriculum
which was centred on a deficit interpretation of learning
difficulties. Accordingly, behavioural perspectives began to
dominate the curriculum design and teaching methods of special
education.

A behavioural objectives approach

This approach does not emphasize the within-child factors that
might contribute to learning difficulty. Instead, it directs attention towards an analysis of the skills that children need in order
to learn specific tasks, and the sequence in which these might be
acquired. From a behavioural perspective, all behaviour is
learned in ways which are governed both by the setting in which
it arises and also by the consequences that follow. The evidence
that learning has occurred takes the form of a change in
observable behaviour. Thus, the focus is placed on what learners
demonstrate that they can do after learning, and no attempt is
made to interpret their inner experiences or cognitive
strategies. When applied to curriculum design, the behavioural
approach draws on Tyler's (1949) principle that the objectives
or intended learning outcomes of teaching should be defined
with sufficient clarity that teachers can assess through direct
observation whether or not they have been met.

Solity and Bull (1987) have described the stages involved in
curriculum development when it is based on a behavioural
model. First, selected subject areas are broken down into units of
study: in one of their examples, for instance, mathematics might
incorporate units dealing with the language of instruction,
problem-solving, money, time, addition, subtraction and so on.
Then the goal of each unit of study is identified and expressed in
behavioural terms, that is, as a precise statement of what a pupil
will do in order to demonstrate that a skill has been learned.
These statements are referred to as behavioural objectives, and
are characterized by:

(i) the use of observable verbs, such as 'write', 'select' and *precise*

'name', rather than non-observable verbs such as 'know', 'understand' or 'appreciate';

(ii) a description of the conditions in which the pupil will demonstrate the skill, such as 'when presented with two sets of objects' or 'within ten minutes'; and

(iii) a specification of the criteria upon which his or her performance will be judged to be successful, such as 'to within two millimetres of accuracy on nine out of ten occasions'.

Thus, for example, the goal of one unit in geography might be described as 'locating and identifying features on a map'. Translated into a behavioural objective, this could become:

Given an OS map at a scale of 1:50,000, the pupil will: (i) locate on the map the points identified by five grid references; (ii) name the features represented by the symbols at those points on three consecutive occasions with 100 per cent accuracy.

The next stage is to analyse the component skills that are necessary in order to attain each objective, again expressing them in behavioural terms. These components should then be sequenced into steps through which the pupil can progress towards achieving the objective. A number of examples of such skills analyses have been published for use by schools (e.g. Ainscow and Tweddle 1979, 1984), and some LEAs have adapted and developed these further. The approach relies heavily on the view that, by comparison with others, children with learning difficulties need more structured and detailed planning of the curricular opportunities that are made available to them, and benefit from clearly expressed and finely graded steps in their learning. As a general rule, the more extensive a pupil's learning difficulties, the smaller each step in the sequence will be.

It can be seen that the behavioural objectives approach focuses on what pupils will do as a result of their learning. It emphasizes detailed planning in which intended learning outcomes are clearly specified in advance. Accordingly, it has widely been acknowledged to promote precise and purposeful curriculum design. A particular strength is in the basis it provides for continuous monitoring and evaluation of a pupil's progress towards the stated objectives. Further, it implies a positive view of pupil learning, because any lack of progress is not attributed to fixed or inherent learner characteristics, but rather to the need to revise and modify some aspect of the curriculum in order to ensure that difficulties are overcome. Considerable success has been reported in the use of a behaviourally based curriculum for the teaching of basic skills, such as literacy and numeracy, to pupils with a wide range of special educational needs. Moreover, the clarity with which objectives are formulated allows for easy communication between teachers and colleagues, parents and the pupils themselves about expectations, progress and attainment.

However, a number of criticisms have been raised about the approach. There is no doubt that behavioural objectives are easier to determine in some areas of the curriculum than others. Specifically, they are most readily applied to 'skills' rather than to aspects of knowledge and understanding. Further, they may only be relevant to certain forms of learning, for it is not always possible or desirable to specify the exact nature of the intended outcomes in advance. The attempt to do so can constrain the opportunities for more open-ended learning activities, in which pupils are encouraged to develop their own problem-solving strategies. A narrow focus on the 'products' of learning can serve to distract attention from the processes that are involved, and this in turn may lead to pupils being viewed as passive recipients of teaching rather than as active participants in the learning process. Thus, as Barnes (1982) has argued, while specific behavioural objectives play an important role in curriculum planning, they represent a 'bad fit' in those aspects where the pupils' own contribution to their learning is of particular significance.

It has generally been acknowledged, therefore, even by some of those who initially espoused the approach (e.g. Ainscow and Tweddle 1988), that where behavioural principles are the sole influence on curriculum development this is likely to lead to a restricted and arid range of learning opportunities, in which the acquisition of basic skills is given an inappropriate priority over other equally important areas of experience. As a result of these concerns, there has been a move in special education towards what Brennan (1985) has described as an 'extended objectives' approach.

An extended objectives approach

An extended objectives approach seeks to balance the rigour in planning and effectiveness in teaching specified skills that is associated with behavioural perspectives with an equally explicit focus on the opportunities that are provided for self-expression, problem-solving and self-directed learning. That is, it aims to address the question not only of what pupils are to do as a result of their learning, but also of the processes by which they are to be actively involved in extending their knowledge, skills and understanding. This implies that curriculum planning must focus on the strategies that teachers use to promote learning, as well as on the content of what they teach.

An emphasis on the processes of learning is associated with the work of Stenhouse (1975). He stressed that learning activities should be designed which were of intrinsic value to pupils, rather than simply the means to achieve predetermined ends. Accordingly, these should be planned in such a way that pupils at different levels of understanding would be able to experience success. Some have argued that his 'process model' lends itself to a more flexible curriculum design for those with special educational needs than the behavioural objectives approach (Goddard 1983, Thomas and Feiler 1988). That is, a greater responsiveness to the full range of pupils' needs may be possible where the emphasis is placed on individual aims and goals rather than on set criteria of success and failure in meeting fixed objectives.

This may well be so. However, the more that outcomes are seen to be open-ended and sometimes unpredictable, the greater the difficulty for a teacher in assessing what pupils have taken from their curricular experiences, and therefore in planning for continuity and progression in their learning. This is necessary for all pupils, and it can be argued that it is even more important where their rate of progress is uneven or slow. It has been increasingly accepted, therefore, that what is required in curriculum planning is a balanced combination of behavioural objectives together with others which are equally carefully structured, but which provide more flexible opportunities for the development of problem-solving and self-expression in pupils' learning. Through this means, explicit attention can be given to social, emotional and cognitive processes in learning, as well as to the more overt signs of achievement (Brennan 1985).

Wider perspectives

The discussion so far has centred on formal aspects of curriculum design, but it should be acknowledged that the relationship between the learning opportunities that are planned and intended and the actual experiences of individual pupils is a complex one. An 'ecological' perspective on children's development and learning emphasizes the ways in which individuals both influence and are influenced by the different learning environments that they experience, and by the relationships between these. Such a perspective has significant implications for curriculum development, for it highlights the importance for pupils' progress of the relationships that exist, not only between the learning contexts of home, school and community, but also within the school itself (Thomas and Feiler 1988). Thus the effects of school organization, pupil groupings and the quality of staff, pupil and staff–pupil relationships on the way in which the curriculum is experienced should all be taken into account. From this standpoint, it can be argued that it may be through adaptations to the climate for learning, as much as through modifications of specific tasks and activities, that the curricular needs of pupils with special educational needs may best be met.

Balance and differentiation in the curriculum

The different approaches to curriculum development that have been outlined here can be seen to vary in the emphasis they give to special educational aims, precisely defined learning outcomes, processes and the context of relationships within which learning takes place. It seems reasonable to suppose that a balanced curriculum should incorporate explicit attention to all these aspects, for it is unlikely that any one approach could meet all the needs of pupils with learning difficulties. Where special educational aims associated with specific impairments to learning are required, these should be integrated as fully as possible within the general framework of the common curriculum. The appropriate balance between specialized and 'normal' curricular experiences may vary for different pupils, but the principle of maximum possible access to the mainstream curriculum should apply. It is important to remember though, that, on the whole, the better the quality of the curriculum for all pupils the less likely it is that many additional or alternative aims will be required. However, it is widely accepted that pupils who experience learning difficulties will need more time than their peers if they are to achieve success in some areas of their learning, and this has implications for the priority that is allocated to these areas within the curriculum.

Literacy and numeracy skills are highly valued in our society and therefore it is not surprising that, prior to the introduction of the National Curriculum, many schools restricted the breadth of the curriculum that was made available to pupils with learning difficulties in order to concentrate attention on the teaching of these skills. However, while it was an understandable response to the practical problems of time management that are associated with meeting special educational needs, it could result in regrettable consequences. For example, a narrow focus on areas of difficulty can often lead to both boredom and frustration. It can also result in a lowering of morale, because fewer opportunities are made available in which pupils might develop areas of relative strength.

There is, then, a dilemma for teachers in the balance they seek between acknowledging and responding to a pupil's special educational needs while at the same time trying to ensure that he or she has access to the full range of curricular experiences. Brennan (1985) has proposed that one way forward is to distinguish between different forms of learning within the curriculum, which he characterizes as 'functional' and 'contextual'. He describes functional learning as that which is judged essential for a pupil: as such, it must be accurate, permanent, thorough and proficient. By contrast, contextual learning allows a pupil to relate to the 'natural, social, emotional and aesthetic' aspects of his or her environment. Thus it involves awareness, familiarity, recognition and appreciation. At first glance, this may simply appear to represent a more sophisticated gloss on the traditional dichotomy between 'the basics' and other aspects of the curriculum. However, Brennan argues that functional and contextual learning should be viewed as interactive and complementary elements of a pupil's learning experience. That is, the skills and knowledge acquired in the former should be drawn upon in more open-ended and self-expressive activities. These, because of their emphasis on achievements of personal relevance to the pupil, may in turn give more sense of purpose and motivation to functional learning. The balance between functional and contextual learning will vary both from pupil to pupil and over time, according to needs and progress, but a central principle here is that the more restricted a pupil's achievements in functional areas of learning, the broader and more important the contextual aspects must become. It may be seen, therefore, that Brennan is advocating a rather different balance of curricular experiences from that which has traditionally been provided. Furthermore, his perspective demonstrates that the notion of balance in the curriculum is intimately bound up with the concept of differentiation.

The consideration of differentiation is not unique to pupils with special educational needs, for it concerns the means by which the curriculum can be adapted in such a way that learning activities are made meaningful and relevant to all pupils, and offer each the opportunity to experience success. Thus it can be seen to be central to effective teaching. Where the curriculum has been designed to meet the full range of pupils' needs as far as possible, then fewer adaptations will be required for individuals or groups, but at the same time any that are necessary should be easier to accommodate. It is implicit within the concept of special educational need, however, that some pupils require additional help if they are to benefit fully from the learning opportunities that are generally provided.

Further, those with the most extensive difficulties will require the greatest attention to flexible adaptations to objectives, teaching approaches and organizational arrangements. It is, therefore, possible to describe a continuum of increasingly differentiated curricular provision which parallels the continuum of special educational need.

Common curriculum with additional support as needed

The National Curriculum Council notes that:

> schools that successfully meet the demands of a diverse range of individual needs through agreed policies on teaching and learning approaches are invariably effective in meeting special educational needs.
>
> (NCC 1989a: para. 5)

If there is flexibility in the pace at which pupils are required to learn, and if work is matched to variation in learning styles, interests, experience and attainment, then the majority of those with special educational needs are not likely to require further differentiation of the curriculum.

To this end, the National Curriculum Council stresses that schools should draw up their curriculum plans in such a way as to ensure that curricular breadth is accessible to all pupils and, further, that a consideration of special educational needs should be integral to the design of the schemes of work that form the core of the curriculum. In implementing these, there should be explicit attention to the balance between individualized and group work, to flexible pupil groupings and to a varied range of teaching methods and materials. Full use should also be made of whatever support is available from parents, colleagues and other professionals. A basic principle they put forward is 'for access to the curriculum to be facilitated by whatever means necessary to ensure that success is achieved' (NCC 1989a: para. 6). For some pupils, this will involve the provision of additional support in the form of special aids and equipment, and others may require supplementary teaching assistance on an individual or small group basis. Where the common curriculum has been designed with all the pupils in mind, however, further differentiation should only be necessary for the minority whose needs cannot fully be met through these means.

Common curriculum with partial modification

For those pupils with specific impairments that impede or restrict their access to general learning opportunities, additional educational aims may necessarily be incorporated into their curriculum. For example, blind children will need teaching in the use of Braille and other tactile aids to their learning, and those with significant language difficulties are likely to need specific programmes to develop their functional communication skills. When this is the case, decisions must be made about the relative priority of special and common educational aims, because time spent on the former inevitably has implications across the rest of the curriculum. As far as possible, the attempt should be made to integrate special aims into mainstream learning experiences, but if specialized needs are to be met effectively then this is likely to involve some modification or reduction in the rest of the pupil's curriculum. Here, the question of relevance is often raised. For example, how relevant is it to a pupil with physical impairment to be included in PE lessons? How relevant is it for a blind pupil to have access to the visual arts programme or for a pupil with specific language difficulties to have the opportunity to learn French? Such questions are not as easily answered as some have suggested, and require collaborative decision-making and continuous reassessment and review. With good reason it may be argued that no area of the curriculum should automatically be regarded as being of little relevance to a pupil with particular special educational needs.

Far more frequent than the addition to or modification of educational aims in order to meet special educational needs, however, are modifications to the ways in which pupils are helped to access the curriculum. These may include the sorts of adaptation to curricular tasks and activities, teaching methods and organizational strategies that are addressed in the following chapter. Whatever form they take, the underlying aim must be to build on pupils' strengths, as well as help overcome areas of difficulty.

Modified common curriculum

Where pupils' learning difficulties extend across most areas of the curriculum, they are likely to require even more explicit attention to the ways in which their needs can be met, while at the same time ensuring that they maintain as much common ground with their peers as possible. This will include, for example, careful consideration of the level at which tasks are set, the presentation and balance of activities, and the degree and style of assistance that will best facilitate their learning and thus ensure progress.

Wholly or partly special curriculum

Finally, in those cases where individual needs are such that it is judged that special goals should take priority in a child's education, then a wholly or partly alternative curriculum may be provided. It should be emphasized though that if it is accepted that the general aims of education are the same for all children (DES 1978, NCC 1989b), then it follows that any necessary alternatives should be developed in ways which are consistent with this principle.

The National Curriculum for children with special educational needs

As discussed in Chapter 2, many commentators have pointed out that children with special educational needs were not explicitly considered when the framework for the National Curriculum was first drawn up. Indeed, at one point it was intended that those with statements of special educational need would automatically be excluded from its provisions. However, it has been acknowledged now that such exclusion would run contrary to the principles of the 1981 Education Act. Accordingly, it is expected that there will be very few formal modifications to or exceptions from the National Curriculum, even among those children who are the subjects of statements.

Despite the lack of specific attention to their needs, in some ways the National Curriculum can be regarded as an important step forward for those with learning difficulties, because their entitlement to a common curriculum with their peers should serve to emphasize the continuum between 'special' and 'ordinary' educational provision. However, while some guidance has been provided on ways in which access to the National Curriculum can be facilitated for pupils with learning difficulties (NCC 1989b), it is evident that the responsibility for ensuring that this is to their benefit rests with individual schools and their teachers. This requires that schools are alert to the potential strengths and limitations of the National Curriculum for children with special educational needs.

Its potential strengths lie in its emphasis on detailed planning, monitoring of progress and curricular breadth. As previously discussed, the National Curriculum Council recommends a whole school approach to planning programmes of study which takes explicit account of special educational needs. If its advice is followed, then this may do much to promote the view that all staff share responsibility for the educational progress of all their pupils. Further, the National Curriculum necessitates a school-wide approach to continuous assessment, together with a detailed system of record-keeping which is shared with both pupils and their parents. Ideally, this can serve to heighten awareness of and responsiveness to individual needs. The implementation of the National Curriculum should have a similarly positive impact too on the breadth of curricular opportunities that are made available to all pupils.

The question of balance in the curriculum, however, remains problematic. Cross-curricular themes, together with explicit attention to personal and social aspects of learning, represent particularly important components of the education of those with special educational needs. Yet it is still unclear how far these can be accommodated within the timetabling constraints that result from the statutory subject-based programmes of study. Further, where there are concerns that the performance of children with learning difficulties may depress a school's average scores on Standard Assessment Tasks, it is understandable that teachers might feel under pressure to give most time and attention to those subjects that are to be formally assessed, at the expense of a more balanced approach to the curriculum. There are, then, grounds for concern that a rigid approach to the delivery of the National Curriculum is unlikely fully to meet pupils' needs.

As far as differentiation of the curriculum is concerned, it has been argued that this is easier to achieve when learning activities have been designed with the full range of pupils' needs in mind. The way in which schools plan their implementation and monitoring of the National Curriculum programmes of study is, therefore, of crucial importance. There is no doubt that flexible planning will be required if the goals of curriculum continuity and progression are to be achieved for all pupils. The National Curriculum Council (1989b) has recommended that this should involve attention to the way in which learning activities can be presented through a sequence of smaller structured steps, in order to ensure that success is achievable for those who find learning difficult.

Such an approach has been identified earlier in this chapter with an objectives model of curriculum planning. Important though it is, however, it is not sufficient to focus only on the nature of the learning activities and the way in which pupils will be expected to engage with these. Rather, as emphasized by the proponents of a broader 'ecological' perspective, it is also necessary to give careful consideration to the contexts that will be provided for learning. Accordingly, the National Curriculum Council has stressed the importance of balance between individual and co-operative group learning, and the quality of teacher–pupil and pupil–pupil relationships, in meeting special educational needs. Organizational arrangements, such as the grouping of pupils who are working at levels of the National Curriculum which fall outside their chronological Key Stage, will require sensitive planning. Finally, the Council emphasizes that, if the curriculum is to be successfully implemented, then explicit attention will need to be given to staff co-operation and co-ordination within school, and to effective forms of liaison with parents, support agencies and the wider school community (NCC 1989b).

Curricular issues are central in special education for when the curriculum is not planned in such a way as to be responsive to individual variation, then learning difficulties will almost inevitably result. For this reason, writers such as Swann (1988b) have warned that 'access' to the curriculum is not necessarily a helpful way of looking at children's needs: rather, it may be that the curriculum itself is in need of change. While the finer detail of the National Curriculum may indeed change over time, there seems little doubt that its framework will remain in place for the foreseeable future. The challenge for teachers is to try to ensure that the entitlement to participation in the National Curriculum results in positive learning experiences for all their pupils, including those with special educational needs.

Discussion points

1 What would you see as the most important issues for teachers if they are to ensure that pupils with special educational needs benefit from their access to the National Curriculum?
2 How far can and should the consideration of individual needs take priority over common needs in curriculum planning? What dilemmas are involved in meeting pupils' special needs while at the same time ensuring that they have the opportunity to participate in the full range of curricular activities available to their peers?
3 'Behavioural objectives are easier to determine in some areas of the curriculum than others.' Consider which areas of the curriculum these might be, and discuss the main strengths and limitations of the approach.

Further reading

Brennan, W. K. (1985) *Curriculum for Special Needs*, Milton Keynes: Open University Press.
NCC (1989b) *Curriculum Guidance 2: A Curriculum for All*, York: NCC.

5 Teaching approaches and organizational strategies

Within any class group, there is considerable variation between pupils in their style and rate of learning, and in their educational attainments. If learning activities are to be made meaningful, relevant and attainable for all pupils, then it is central to a teacher's task to find ways to respond to that diversity, and this is true whether or not some of the pupils are judged to have special educational needs. The more extensive a particular pupil's learning difficulties, the more apparent will be the need for carefully planned adaptations to the general teaching approach. However, the principles that underlie these adaptations are the same across the full range of individual pupil variation. That is, while it should not be denied that specialist methods may be required for those with specific impairments, it is important to emphasize that, on the whole, children with special educational needs learn from teaching approaches which are also effective for their peers. Thus it is difficult to make a qualitative distinction between 'special' and 'ordinary' practice. Rather, it can be argued that where children have special educational needs, this requires us to look more closely at those factors that we understand to promote effective learning for all children: from this perspective, the needs of children with learning difficulties are for 'good' educational practice.

Classroom-based assessment

Pupils with special educational needs show as great a range of individual variation as their peers, and accordingly individual classroom-based assessment must be the starting point for determining the type and degree of assistance that will help

Does the pupil:
1 Accept familiar tasks willingly?
2 Accept unfamiliar tasks willingly?
3 Start tasks immediately?
4 Ask for help if appropriate?
5 Only begin tasks if understands?
6 Show motivation to complete tasks?
7 Resist distractions?
8 Cope with task frustrations?
9 Complete tasks in given time?

Figure 5.1 An extract from a comprehensive school's screening checklist for pupils' task-related behaviour

them build on existing strengths and overcome areas of difficulty. Special educational needs are interactive in nature, and therefore it is important for teachers to gather information not only about pupils' relative strengths and weaknesses, but also about how these interact with the learning demands of the classroom. An individual pupil's approach to learning will vary in the contexts of different tasks and activities, organizational strategies, teaching methods and classroom relationships. The aim of classroom-based assessment, therefore, must be to attempt to analyse the way in which a pupil's skills, knowledge and understanding interact with these aspects of the classroom environment (Norwich 1990).

Such an assessment will entail both direct observation and also individual discussion with the pupils. It is useful first to gather general observational evidence of their responses to classroom routines, tasks and relationships. Particular concerns here might include the degree to which they demonstrate initiative and self-management in their learning, for example, by organizing their own materials, maintaining attention to tasks, and knowing when and how to seek help (Westwood 1987). Teachers sometimes find it helpful to adopt checklists of questions in order to structure their observations. For example, Figure 5.1 shows part of a pupil behaviour checklist which was drawn up by a special needs co-ordinator in a comprehensive school for use by his colleagues.

Comparisons of the observations made of individual pupils in different classroom activities should reveal any variations in their approach to learning which are associated with particular sorts of task demands and learning contexts. From these initial observations it may also often be the case that questions arise which merit more systematic investigation. These might include, for example, how often a pupil seeks teacher reassurance during lessons or how much of the allocated time a pupil actually spends engaged with a set task, and whether this differs according to the type of activity or pupil grouping. The answers to questions of this kind can alert teachers to factors that appear to contribute to a pupil's difficulty.

If pupils are to be helped to achieve progress and success in their learning, then this necessitates close monitoring of their level of grasp of the skills, knowledge and concepts required by specific curricular tasks. Observations of their general approach to learning must therefore be complemented by more focused curriculum-based assessment. This should not only involve an evaluation of the work produced, but also direct observations of the way in which the pupils engage with the task. For those experiencing difficulties, it is valuable to compare what can be done independently with what can be done when provided with varying degrees of help. Further, through individual discussion, it is also important to try to find out the pupils' own perceptions of the purpose of the task and their explanations of the strategies they used in carrying it out. Lewis (1991) suggests that, both in their observations and discussions, key concerns for teachers must include the extent to which pupils understand what they have been asked to do, the nature of any consistent error patterns in their work, and how successfully they have retained and used earlier learning in their approach to the task.

It should be apparent that the assessment process outlined above is not confined to children with special educational needs. The National Curriculum provides a framework for continuous curriculum-based assessment for all pupils, and SEAC (1990) has issued guidance for teachers on the way in which this might be carried out. However, it is of particular importance for those experiencing difficulties in their learning, for as SEAC has pointed out:

Careful assessment, of a formal and informal kind, has always been a hallmark of good practice across the range of special educational needs . . . [because] in order to judge the pace and progression of learning, regular and often frequent checks on a pupil's acquisition of knowledge, understanding and skill are necessary.

(cited by NCC 1989b)

There is no doubt that regular and detailed observational assessment is time-consuming. If it is to be valuable to both teachers and pupils, therefore, it should help inform planning for teaching. That is, the evidence gathered should enable teachers:

(i) to determine priorities and starting points for learning;
(ii) to form hypotheses about factors in the interaction between pupil and learning environment which assist or hinder progress; and
(iii) to identify the sorts of flexible adaptation that might best help the pupil to achieve success.

Once these adaptations have been introduced, then continuous assessment and detailed record-keeping of pupil progress should allow their effectiveness to be monitored and reviewed.

The discussion so far has been focused on the central role of the class teacher in the assessment process. However, the role of the pupil should also be considered, as there is a considerable consensus of opinion concerning the importance of involving pupils as fully as possible in self-evaluation and monitoring of their own progress. Wolfendale (1987) has argued that teachers have a responsibility to help all children to:

understand the point and purpose of the learning tasks presented to them and in which they engage;
learn how to learn;
evolve effective learning strategies;
identify learning hurdles, 'sticking points' along the way, and apply appropriate problem-solving learning strategies.

(Wolfendale 1987: 37)

Such a perspective highlights the need to foster children's active involvement in and reflection on their own learning, including the assessment of their strengths, weaknesses, achievements and learning needs. Children with learning difficulties have sometimes been characterized as passive learners, but it seems reasonable to suppose that more purposeful and active engagement with their learning might be made easier if they are enabled to see clearly for what they are aiming and why, when they are helped to see how this builds upon and takes further their existing knowledge, skills and experience, and when they are encouraged to monitor their progress through the various steps towards achieving their learning goals. It might be added, too, that pupils may well have their own perceptions of the sorts of assistance that would meet their needs.

For a more complete assessment profile of a pupil, of course, classroom-based assessment will need to be complemented by information from other sources, including other school staff and, where appropriate, support agencies from educational and other services. The potential contribution of the pupil's parents must be considered here, for they represent a unique source of information about their child's interests, learning experiences and social interactions, both at home and in other out-of-school contexts. They can also have important insights to offer about their child's response to school, and about the type of strategies that might be most effective in overcoming areas of difficulty. Significantly, these strategies may entail closer home–school co-operation and a joint approach to facilitating the child's learning, for, as the Warnock Committee (DES 1978) commented, there is little doubt that where parents and teachers work together collaboratively, this is to the benefit of the children concerned. The support that a class teacher may draw on from colleagues, other professionals and parents is discussed more fully in Chapter 7.

Adaptations to curricular tasks and activities

A major concern in the planning of curricular tasks and activities is that these should be sufficiently well matched to pupils' existing learning as to ensure continuity and progression. This implies that planning should take account of diversity in both pace and level of learning. Children with special educational needs are almost invariably described as slow to complete certain types of set work and, therefore, if they are to experience the sense of achievement that derives from the satisfactory completion of a varied and balanced range of curricular activities, this has implications for the design of tasks which can realistically be undertaken in the time that is allocated.

Pace of learning is, of course, partly associated with the provision of realistic learning demands. Some children may experience difficulty in perceiving what is required of them, and in understanding what strategies they need to apply. Accordingly, they can appear to be distracted by irrelevant aspects of the activity, and adopt what to an outsider may seem an unsystematic approach to the task. Difficulties are particularly likely to arise in those tasks that involve abstract or complex ideas, where the step between their existing learning and what is required may simply be too large to take without additional assistance.

It is important, therefore, that in their planning teachers attempt to analyse quite explicitly the skills, knowledge and problem-solving strategies involved in particular tasks, and that they use their curriculum-based assessments to identify what, if any, gaps in learning or other hurdles pupils will need help to overcome. Where their existing levels of learning are such that the task demands are too great, pupils are likely to benefit from a more structured set of activities designed to enable them to progress step by step towards their curriculum goals. The size of each step or 'intermediate goal' (NCC 1989b) should be carefully matched so that it is within pupils' reach but is sufficiently stretching to challenge and motivate them.

In some cases the setting of intermediate goals can be informed by the sort of task analysis associated with an objectives-based approach to the curriculum described in the previous chapter. In this, an attempt is made to specify and sequence the skills and knowledge a pupil needs in order to achieve the longer term curriculum goal, and to use the resulting analysis as a basis for developing a set of activities through which they can be taught. However, task analysis has its limitations: it is more readily applied to some areas of the curriculum than others and, even where it is possible to describe a 'logical' sequence of steps, it should be borne in mind that pupils learn by different routes. Accordingly it is rarely possible to specify in advance a single 'correct' progression that will be effective for all learners. Nevertheless, the underlying principles can be used with some flexibility, and the attempt to analyse a specific task as precisely as possible is a valuable aid to more structured curriculum planning.

In addition to the structuring of curricular tasks, attention in planning may also need to be given to the opportunities that are provided for pupils to practise and consolidate recently developed learning. Pupils with learning difficulties are often characterized as having a poor memory for newly acquired knowledge and skills, and where this is so they will need curricular experiences which allow them actively to rehearse these. To be effective in helping them consolidate their learning, though, it is not sufficient to require pupils to continue to repeat the same inaccurately completed exercise until they 'get it right'. Rather, activities will be needed which enable them to review previous learning in a range of purposeful and interesting contexts.

Furthermore, if pupils are to make the best functional use of the knowledge, skills and learning strategies that they have acquired they need to recognize how these can be generalized and applied in adaptable ways to novel learning situations. Thus, for example, in the early stages of their mathematical learning they will need to learn that the same strategies are involved in counting or in adding, regardless of the materials (e.g. bricks, books, sweets, people) that are to be used. Later, they will need to learn that they can apply computational strategies flexibly to problems such as: $5 + 3 = ?$; $5 + ? = 8$; or even, 'I should have eight felt tip pens, but I can only find five. . .'; and so on. The ease with which learners are able to make such generalizations, and the flexibility with which they adapt to novel problem-solving tasks, will partly depend on how complete a grasp they have of the necessary strategies as well as on how confident they feel in their use of these. However, it is important for teachers to be aware that many pupils with learning difficulties appear to need help in applying their skills to new learning contexts. It will be necessary, therefore, to plan specific activities which will facilitate this.

It can be seen, then, that in order to meet the full range of pupils' needs, adaptations may be required in the pacing and structure of intermediate goals, the provision of additional consolidation activities and the degree of explicit planning to promote generalization. For pupils with special educational needs, if their motivation for learning is to be enhanced and maintained, a guiding principle in planning must be to provide the sort of practical and active tasks that build on their strengths, interests and first-hand experiences. Further, it is important to emphasize that no matter how much structured help and guidance may be required for certain tasks pupils with learning difficulties also need the same range and variety in their curricular experiences, including opportunities for open-ended learning, choice and self-direction, as their peers.

Teaching methods

From the preceding discussion it should be clear that while adaptations to curricular tasks and activities have a very important role to play in helping pupils overcome learning difficulties they represent only one aspect of the planning that may be necessary in order to meet the full range of individual educational needs. In this section, attention is drawn to some of the teaching methods that can be employed to support pupils' learning. A distinction is drawn between methods that are involved prior to pupils' engagement with a curricular task and the support that can be given during this.

It can be argued that the preparation of materials to support pupils' learning is a particularly significant aspect of the teacher's role in responding to special educational needs. Furthermore, it entails the sort of advanced planning that can only be of benefit to all pupils (Hodgson 1989). Few pupils will require specialized aids or equipment in their learning, but where, for example, a visually impaired pupil requires material to be produced in enlarged print, Braille or on tape, then this clearly necessitates making arrangements well in advance. More generally, though, it is important to recognize that an over-reliance on written material is likely to put many children with learning difficulties at a disadvantage, and therefore other media, such as visual, auditory or tactile aids, should be incorporated where possible. Written materials are, of course, central to much teaching, but published worksheets and textbooks will often require some modification if they are not to present an unnecessary hurdle to particular pupils in their learning. Whether adapting such written material or producing one's own, it will be necessary to pay attention to vocabulary, sentence length and reading level, as well as to the clarity with which information or instructions are sequenced. Print size, page layout and the use of cues to help focus and direct a pupil's reading may be further considerations (see, for example, Lewis 1991). Whatever form these materials take, however, it is particularly important to ensure that they are complemented by the provision of a variety of 'concrete' examples with which pupils can actively engage and derive first-hand practical experience.

The process of preparing materials frequently involves some decisions about the sort of response that will be expected from pupils, and, while certain curricular tasks clearly require a written form of response, others do not. Those children who have difficulty in writing may engage with tasks more enthusiastically and also reveal a great deal more about what they have learned from their activities where they can present this, at least initially, in other ways. These might include, for example, spoken discussion, drawing, role play or practical demonstration, and it should be noted that certain aspects of the National Curriculum assessment do allow for such alternative forms of response for some pupils with special educational needs.

There is no doubt that the clarity with which teachers introduce and present tasks to their pupils has a significant influence on their learning. Ainscow (1989) has suggested that most children who 'don't get on' in lessons appear unaware or uncertain of what it is they are meant to do and why. In order to ensure that all pupils have a clear understanding of the purpose of the learning activities with which they are to engage, it is self-evident that instructions and explanations should be explicit and unambiguous. Thus teachers will need to monitor the language structures and vocabulary that they use, and to modify these according to pupils' responses. It is equally important that they discuss and check pupils' understanding of the strategies that they will need to employ, both before they begin and also once they are working on the task. Attention will therefore need to be given to the sorts of questioning technique that may best elicit information from the pupils concerning their grasp of the task in hand.

Their curriculum-based assessments should alert teachers to which pupils may experience difficulties with the activity and the sort of assistance that will be required if they are to complete it successfully. For those with the most extensive difficulties it may be necessary to plan a structured programme of support, whereby they are helped to progress step by step from full teacher assistance and guidance to increasingly independent learning as they gain in competence and confidence. All pupils with learning difficulties, however, benefit from the provision of regular feedback on how they are progressing, and this necessitates close monitoring by their teachers. Through corrective feedback teachers can help to prevent the development of persistent errors or misconceptions, and through positive feedback they can offer encouragement and reassurance. Where positive feedback is given, it should be as specific as possible, in order to help pupils see exactly how and why their learning strategies have been successful.

Teacher praise is important for all pupils and perhaps particularly so for those with learning difficulties, for it can demonstrate that their achievements are acknowledged and valued. In order to do so, though, praise must be seen to be genuine and to be given for genuine effort. In other circumstances it is unhelpful, for it not only conveys low expectations, but also fails to clarify for the pupil the learning demands of the particular task. Furthermore, it should be noted that there is a fine line to tread in judging what degree of teacher assistance and feedback is appropriate (Westwood 1987). Too little, and a pupil may become frustrated and lose confidence; too much, and the teacher may inadvertently foster undue pupil dependency. It is to the benefit of neither teacher nor pupil if the latter learns to seek continuous reassurance that he or she is 'doing the right thing'. Rather, it would seem preferable to help all pupils develop strategies whereby they can check and review their own work. By doing so, they are likely to gain a clearer understanding of the way in which their own efforts have contributed to their success.

On the whole, the adaptations to teaching methods that have been outlined can be characterized as 'common sense' (Westwood 1987). That is, they primarily involve closer attention to aspects of planning which need to be considered for all pupils. However, if they are to be effective, then they must be used in a consistent and purposeful way. This requires that planning is explicitly informed by careful assessment of the nature of a pupil's difficulties and by close monitoring of his or her progress. More specialized methods are sometimes recommended. These may take the form of individualized or small group programmes, devised by the school's special needs co-ordinator and/or advisory teachers or educational psychologist. Where a pupil's difficulties lie in the acquisition of basic literacy and numeracy skills, for example, programmes are frequently based on a behavioural objectives approach. These will employ more carefully graded materials, more directive and structured teaching techniques, and a finer-grained recording of pupil progress than would ordinarily be needed. Such programmes may be implemented by the class teacher or by support staff, either within or outside the usual classroom context. However, they are usually only adopted in those situations where it is judged that a pupil's difficulties are such as to impede his or her learning progress if more intensive intervention is not provided.

Organizational strategies

The degree of success that pupils experience in their learning is influenced not only by the nature of planned curricular tasks and teaching methods but also by contextual factors within the classroom. These include, for example, its physical organization, the timing and pacing of learning activities, the management of resources to support learning and the grouping of pupils.

A primary concern in considering the physical organization of the classroom must be the range and variety of curricular activities that are to take place there, and how the layout of the room can best facilitate both pupil engagement with these and teacher supervision and guidance of their learning. While attention to lighting, noise level, ease of access to equipment and resources, and mobility between different areas will be necessary in any classroom, it is particularly important where there are pupils with sensory or physical impairments. Further, individual pupils are likely to have different levels of tolerance for what they find distracting in their environment: observational assessment should indicate whether there is a need, for example, for quieter or more sheltered working areas which can be used as required. Caution may be necessary, however, to ensure that these do not result in permanent physical segregation within the classroom of those pupils who find concentration difficult.

Variations in pupils' pace of work, and in the extent of their need for assistance and for repeated practice or consolidation activities, raise significant issues for teachers concerning the management of time and resources. Here, it is not simply a question of the time or resources that are available, but the use to which they are put. It is not unusual to find, as Croll and Moses (1985) did in their study of junior classrooms, that on average children with special educational needs spend less time directly engaged with curricular activities, and correspondingly more time distracted from their work, than do their peers. As these are the very pupils who may be thought to require more time spent on task, this indicates a need for organizational and management strategies which enable maximum opportunities for teacher interaction with pupils and concentrated engagement with learning activities (Ainscow 1989).

This does not imply that pupils with special educational needs necessarily require one-to-one attention from their teacher, although there is no doubt that when this is given their level of task engagement increases significantly. Although special individual learning programmes may be needed by some pupils, these can only form a small part of their curriculum, for no matter how good the programmes are, if pupils spend most of their time in this way they are effectively being segregated from the rest of the class (Lewis 1991). Where there is an absence of common ground and shared learning experiences with peers, this may exacerbate the social difficulties that many children with special educational needs can experience. It is important, therefore, to look at the balance of individual, group and class activities provided for all pupils and, in doing so, to recognize that peers can be a particularly significant learning resource in the classroom.

It is generally acknowledged that peers can act as influential models for each other, and that peer acceptance and approval can be powerful incentives. Their potential teaching role is often used incidentally and informally in classrooms; for example, when one pupil is asked to explain or demonstrate an activity to another. It may, however, be formalized through peer-tutoring schemes (Topping 1988), where pupils are coached in a specific tutoring role such as in reading, and paired with pupils to whom they then give regular individual help. Sometimes pupils are tutors to others in their own class, and sometimes to those who are younger. An interesting development has been in the involvement of older pupils who themselves have reading difficulties as tutors of younger children. Where these schemes have worked well, considerable benefits have been claimed both for those being tutored and also for the tutors, and the pupils have apparently enjoyed the experience. However, if peer tutoring is to be successful, there is clearly a need for sensitivity, not only in the way in which the scheme is introduced but also in assessing which pupils will work constructively together. If pupils are to be tutored by others in their class, it will be important that at other times they are seen to have their own contribution to make to paired or group learning.

In formal peer-tutoring arrangements, it is often reported that the paired pupils develop a mutual sense of purpose and a shared pleasure in achievement, and furthermore that the learning of both is enhanced. However, their relationship is essentially unequal, insofar as one is giving and the other receiving help. By contrast, a unique quality of peer relationships in general is that they involve more equal status than is true of adult–child or teacher–pupil interaction. As a result, peers can not only provide an alternative form of assistance, but can also make different learning demands of one another than those made by teachers. It is, for example, important for the development of their problem-solving strategies that pupils are exposed to alternative viewpoints, articulate, clarify and justify their own, and learn ways of reconciling differences in perspectives. There is some evidence that paired or small group activity may play a particularly important role here. For example, children have been reported to solve certain problems at a more advanced level when working co-operatively in pairs, whether of similar or dissimilar achievement, than when working independently (e.g. Bearison 1983). If it is to be successful, co-operative work requires careful planning, because it entails an additional set of learning demands for the pupils to those that are implicit in the task itself. However, it has been suggested that when it is well managed it can lead not only to improved academic attainment, but also to enhanced self-esteem and social relations (Ainscow 1989).

The recognition of the role peers can play in helping one another's learning has implications for the way in which pupils are organized into groups within the classroom, and, indeed, within the school. Much debate has focused on the relative advantages and disadvantages of different forms of grouping, but the evidence from studies of co-operative learning suggests that, at least for some activities, 'mixed ability' groupings can be of benefit on academic, personal and social grounds. Those who advocate a greater use of mixed ability teaching argue that grouping by ability can adversely affect not only teacher expectations, but also pupils' perceptions of themselves as learners. Further, it may convey a message that attainment, above all, is what is highly valued in the classroom, and may reinforce feelings of failure among those who find learning difficult. These are serious concerns for anyone committed to meeting the full range of pupils' needs. However, there is no doubt that even in mixed ability classes, teachers frequently find that for certain purposes it is a more effective strategy to group by level of attainment. Where this is done, it is, of course, important that the criteria upon which groups are based fit the specific teaching purpose, and that groupings are reviewed and revised in the light of continuous assessment. Whatever organizational arrangements are made, it has been argued that a fundamental principle must be to provide within the classroom, 'an atmosphere of encouragement, acceptance, respect for individual achievements and sensitivity to individual needs, in which all pupils can thrive' (NCC 1989b: 7). The extent to which a teacher is successful in doing this may well prove to be more important than the exact balance of different grouping arrangements which he or she employs. Most, however, would agree with the National Curriculum Council's recommendation that flexible groupings should be adopted to suit different teaching purposes.

A further consideration in meeting the full range of pupils' needs concerns the way in which any additional adult assistance is organized in order to support their learning. Individual pupils with statements of special educational need do in several cases have further help available in the classroom on an hourly or daily basis from designated support assistants. The way in which a class teacher manages this support will vary according to the pupil's particular needs. However, it is unlikely to help the pupil's social or functional integration and independence in the classroom if the support assistant is always engaged in a one-to-one supervisory role. Increasingly, therefore, it has been accepted that supplementary assistance of this kind should be managed flexibly if it is to enhance the learning opportunities that are provided. There is, though, rather more argument regarding the most appropriate organization of specialist or additional teacher help for those experiencing learning difficulties. Here, the central issue has been whether it should be given by 'in-class support' or by sessional withdrawal of pupils from the classroom, and accordingly this involves school policy rather more than the individual decisions of particular teachers.

The use of in-class support has been associated with a whole school approach to provision for pupils with special educational needs, because it can be argued that it should ensure that all class teachers maintain responsibility for their learning. By contrast, when a withdrawal system is operated, this responsibility may be seen as solely resting with the staff who support the pupils outside the classroom. It has frequently been suggested that withdrawal can lead to pupils being negatively labelled, although it should be pointed out that this may also result from visible and identifiably 'special' support within the classroom. Perhaps most significantly, however, poorly timed and badly co-ordinated withdrawal can result in considerable disruption to a pupil's learning in other curricular activities. Thus, for example, pupils may be withdrawn from lessons in which they could develop real strengths, or may miss the practical sessions which they return to find the rest of their class discussing. Where there is little or no co-ordination between support teacher and class teachers, and scant attention to the way in which classwork and support work should be integrated, then clearly withdrawal must be viewed as unsatisfactory. However, a more positive system of withdrawal is possible, and when flexibly used need not be incompatible with a whole school approach.

For this to be the case, withdrawal will be characterized by regular joint planning and review between all the teachers concerned, so that the support pupils receive is followed through into the classroom. Further, the withdrawal sessions will be sensitively timed in order to minimize disruption and to ensure that pupils still benefit from the full range of curricular experiences (Gipps, Gross and Goldstein 1987). Some children are likely to find it easier to concentrate on particular sorts of support activity in a quiet withdrawal room, and feel more comfortable asking for help and guidance in a smaller group context. In such circumstances, or where the support activities themselves might be disruptive to the rest of the class, then withdrawal can be an effective strategy. In other situations, though, in-class support allows greater potential flexibility in the way class teacher and support teacher work together, and the assistance given to the pupil can more readily be integrated with the curricular activities of the rest of the class. In-class support does, however, require considerable commitment to co-operative planning and teaching from all the staff concerned. Whichever approach or combination of approaches is adopted, if it is to be of optimal value to the pupil, then as Gipps and her colleagues (1987) have pointed out, it is the quality of the support rather than where it takes place that must be the prime concern.

Classroom relationships

An emphasis on the importance of positive and co-operative classroom relationships, both between teachers and pupils and between the pupils themselves, has been implicit in much of the preceding discussion. There is a complex interaction between personal, social and more academic aspects of learning and it is not surprising to find that pupils who experience problems with the demands made by the formal curriculum in school may often also demonstrate difficulties in their personal and social relationships. The National Curriculum Council has suggested that pupils with special educational needs may have even stronger needs than others for positive and supportive attitudes from staff, and for the provision of a classroom climate in which 'all pupils feel valued and able to risk making mistakes as they learn, without fear of criticism' (NCC 1989b: 8).

In schools and classrooms where expectations of children with special educational needs are low, and they both perceive themselves and are seen by their peers as failures, this is likely to have a negative effect not only on their self-esteem and confidence, but also on their enthusiasm and motivation for learning and for co-operation with others. By contrast, positive expectations and confidence in themselves as learners may do much to promote their achievements, and in learning environments where their efforts and achievements are recognized and genuinely valued, their personal and social development can be enhanced. A more detailed consideration of the social and emotional climate of classroom relationships forms the focus of the next chapter.

Discussion points

1 Select a task which you would plan for a group of pupils. Then (i) attempt to analyse the skills, knowledge and concepts that the task requires; and (ii) outline a sequence of

activities through which these might be taught. Consider the strengths and limitations of this form of task analysis as an aid to planning.

2 Use your analysis as a framework for considering what sorts of assessment evidence you would need in order to establish appropriate starting points for teaching the selected task, and to identify potential areas of difficulty that pupils might experience.

3 Lewis (1991) has argued that there is little merit in pretending that differences in attainment do not exist, for the pupils will certainly be aware of them. With respect to their classroom relationships and their approach to learning, consider what might be the impact on pupils with special educational needs of 'ability' and 'mixed ability' groupings.

Further reading

Lewis, A. (1991) *Primary Special Needs and the National Curriculum*, London: Routledge.

Ramasut, A. (ed.) (1989) *Whole School Approaches to Special Needs: A Practical Guide for Secondary Teachers*, Lewes: Falmer.

Westwood, P. (1987) *Commonsense Methods for Children with Special Needs*, London: Croom Helm.

6 The social and emotional context for learning

An interactive concept of special educational needs emphasizes that pupils experience difficulties where there is a significant mismatch between what they themselves bring to bear in learning situations and the expectations that are made of them. In the previous chapters, attention has primarily been focused on the learning demands of the formal curriculum. It should be acknowledged, however, that the informal or 'hidden' curriculum of relationships and interactions at school can also pose considerable demands of pupils with respect to their social competence and their personal resources, such as self-confidence. The interrelationships between children's learning achievements and their social and personal development are complex, but it is generally accepted that pupils learn most effectively when they feel valued and secure, trust their teachers, and both understand and accept the full range of classroom demands (Pollard 1988). For all pupils, therefore, there is a need to consider the social context and emotional climate for learning that classrooms and schools provide. However, both the Warnock Committee (DES 1978) and the National Curriculum Council (1989b) have argued that this may be particularly important for those with special educational needs.

Children with learning difficulties

Where children repeatedly experience failure in their learning, this will almost certainly have a negative impact on their self-esteem. They are likely to begin to doubt their own competence as learners, and see any successes they have as arising from factors outside their control. In such situations, they may feel anxious, frustrated and personally helpless, or they may start to view curricular tasks as boring and irrelevant and become disaffected with classroom learning (Galloway 1990). It should not be surprising then if, in order to retain a personal sense of worth, they develop strategies of task avoidance, for example by passive withdrawal from their engagement with learning activities or by more overt distraction and disruption of the work of their peers. However, it must be stressed that it is by no means inevitable that children with learning difficulties should demonstrate such problems. When positive steps are taken to provide appropriate guidance and support, they can be helped to experience regular success, to monitor and gain confidence in their own developing competence, and to see that their achievements are valued. Nevertheless, pupils with learning difficulties are frequently also described by their teachers as showing emotional and behavioural difficulties, and where this is so, it is important to be alert to the potential contribution that can be made by the climate of attitudes, expectations and relationships within the classroom.

Teacher attitudes towards and expectations of pupils, and the extent to which these are communicated, are fundamentally important. They can influence not only the way in which individual pupils perceive themselves, but also the way that they are viewed by their peers. The attitudes and behaviour that teachers demonstrate towards pupils with learning difficulties are, as discussed previously, affected by a range of factors. These will include their knowledge, information and understanding of special educational needs, their confidence in their own professinal competence to meet the full range of those needs, and the quality and availability of any necessary additional support. However, it would appear central to the development of a positive attitude that, first, needs are recognized as predominantly interactive in nature, rather than as fixed and unchangeable characteristics of a child, and, second, that while individual differences are acknowledged and respected, these are neither unnecessarily emphasized nor allowed to result in an inappropriate lowering of expectations.

If teachers are to plan and organize their teaching in a way which is responsive to individual need, they do of course need to develop differential expectations of different pupils. What seems most important, though, is that these expectations are founded on accurate information and are realistically high. Further, teachers should be aware of the expectations that they hold, and must be prepared to adapt these flexibly on the basis of their continuous assessment. Of course, it is not only the expectations that teachers hold but also the ways in which these are communicated to pupils that are significant. They can be demonstrated both verbally and non-verbally, for example, by the learning tasks teachers set, the feedback they give and the nature of the individual attention they provide.

It has often been argued that children tend to conform to the expectations that are conveyed by their teachers. Low expectations which might be thought likely to have a cumulative adverse effect can be communicated when teachers resort to frequent negative criticism of work. This will be particularly so if the criticism focuses on the pupil as a learner, rather than on task-related guidance as to how he or she might become more successful. By contrast, when teachers give supportive and constructive critical feedback, in which they draw attention to personal effort and progress and acknowledge individual achievement, their strategies may do much to promote pupils' learning. Teacher behaviour which appears positive does not always demonstrate high expectations, however. Laslett and Smith (1984) have pointed out that some well-intentioned teacher responses to individual need can inadvertently act to reinforce a pupil's feelings of inadequacy or difference from his or her peers. They caution that oversimplified questioning, the provision of activities which are obviously different from those for the rest of the class, and the use of indiscriminate praise for inadequate work are often symptomatic of inappropriately low expectations. On the whole, then, it would appear that if teachers are to communicate positive expectations of pupils, this can best be achieved where any necessary adaptations to their teaching approach are made in as unobtrusive a manner as possible, and where attention is focused on individual progress rather than on comparisons with peers.

A positive learning environment, in which all pupils feel that they are valued members of a mutually supportive class group, is fundamentally associated with the quality of relationships within the classroom. This will embrace not only teacher–pupil relationships, but also those among the pupils themselves. Good peer relationships are important for children's personal and social development, and, as discussed in the previous chapter, pupils can act as influential models and tutors for one another's learning. However, it is often pointed out that, in schools and classes where academic attainment and competitiveness are the only predominant values, children with learning difficulties are likely to have poor status among their peers. If teachers wish to foster a classroom climate in which expectations are realistically high, and in which all pupils are respected as individuals and all feel they have a worthwhile contribution to make, it is essential that co-operative aspects of learning and non-academic achievements are also given an appropriate emphasis.

Emotional and behavioural difficulties at school

Within any school there will be some pupils who have greater difficulties than others in meeting the personal and social demands that are made of them. These pupils may need additional help in order to establish positive relationships with their teachers and their peers. They are likely to include, for example, children who feel vulnerable or insecure, those with poorly developed social skills and others who have learned inappropriate strategies for gaining attention (Fontana 1985). Whether they demonstrate their difficulties through passive or more overt forms of behaviour, they can often have a considerable impact on the general climate of classroom relationships. Where their problems in adjusting to the social and personal demands of school persist, and are such as to interfere with their own learning, the learning of their peers or their teacher's organizational and management strategies, they are likely to be identified as having emotional or behavioural difficulties.

It is clear that a wide range of interacting factors can contribute to emotional and behavioural difficulties. These include the child's health and temperament, home and family circumstances and wider community influences. While not denying the significance of these factors, it should, however, be acknowledged that schools and classrooms can also play an important part. It is necessary, therefore, that teachers are alert to those aspects of school life that may influence the difficulties that pupils experience, and, further, that they seek to identify those that might be amenable to change (Galloway 1985).

We may all behave differently in different contexts. Furthermore, any individual might show problematic behaviour in certain situations. It follows, then, that 'difficult' behaviour at school cannot be viewed in isolation from the context in which it occurs. Schools and teachers can vary in the value judgements they bring to bear when defining particular behaviour as problematic, and also in the way they respond to these. There is evidence too that schools vary in their effectiveness in establishing and maintaining appropriate standards of behaviour (Rutter et al. 1979). It has therefore been increasingly recognized that both the formal curriculum and the general ethos of a school can have a considerable impact on pupil behaviour. As a result, attention has been drawn to the need for 'whole school' policies which aim to minimize the likelihood that pupils will experience emotional or behavioural difficulties, and to develop strategies which will alleviate rather than aggravate those problems which do arise. It has been suggested that, on the whole, teachers may be more alert to overt forms of disruption than to signs of emotional withdrawal at school (ILEA 1985). However, a broad-based school policy which is designed to promote positive behaviour should provide a secure learning context which will help all pupils develop their personal resources and social relationships.

The exact form that such a policy takes will obviously vary according to the strengths of the school staff and the needs of the pupils. However, the Elton Committee on discipline in schools (DES 1989c) set out some important principles. It recommends that the pupils themselves should be involved in the process of development and review of school policy, and that there should also be close liaison with their parents as well as with other agencies. The main aim of the policy should be to create a 'positive atmosphere based on a sense of community and a shared sense of values' (p. 13), where rules are clearly communicated and agreed. Explicit consideration should be given in the school curriculum to the development of mutual respect, responsibility and self-discipline: the Committee points out that this necessitates that personal and social as well as academic aspects of learning are monitored, and that the full range of pupils' achievements is given due recognition. However, it emphasizes that no matter how carefully designed the school policy is, its successful implementation will depend on the quality of teacher–pupil relationships and on the establishment of effective classroom management.

Teacher–pupil relationships and classroom management

Positive teacher–pupil relationships are fundamental to effective classroom management, because any strategies a teacher employs will be more successful in a climate of mutual respect. The extent to which teachers demonstrate genuine interest in pupils as individuals, as well as care and concern for the class as a whole, is reflected in their planning, organization and management of learning experiences. It is clear that problematic behaviour is less likely to arise in lessons which maximize pupils' engagement with curricular activities, because this automatically reduces the opportunity for disruption. Planning for this level of task involvement implies an explicit consideration of both individual and full class needs. For example, where pupils have difficulties in peer relationships which interfere with their learning, it is important not only to help them as individuals to develop their confidence and social skills, but also to work with the class as a whole in order to ensure that they do not become the subject of teasing, ridicule or rejection. Similarly, when pupils have learning difficulties, there is a need to promote their self-esteem and their motivation for learning by the provision of relevant and achievable tasks, and by regular constructive feedback and praise. It should be apparent, though, that the value of such strategies is not confined to those with difficulties, for all pupils are likely to show more enthusiasm for and involvement in curricular activities when the full range of personal and co-operative achievements is seen to be positively valued.

In order to establish effective classroom management, however, it is important that teachers should not only provide positive feedback to pupils on their curricular achievements, but also on their behaviour. It is often reported that teachers are generally sparing with their praise for personal and social conduct, and give far more attention to misbehaviour. A positive approach to classroom management (e.g. Galvin, Mercer and Costa 1990) is very different from this, because it is based on the premise that it is more effective to reward the keeping of rules than it is to punish their infringement. From this perspective, pupils need to be clear about what their teachers expect and why, and should receive positive rather than negative feedback to clarify how far they are meeting these expectations. A starting point, therefore, is the establishment of explicit and agreed rules and routines which can be regularly reviewed with the class. These should be framed in positive terms, such as 'we sit quietly in assembly', 'we walk along the corridor', 'we listen when others are talking'. Then, instead of drawing attention to the rules when they are broken, a strategy is used which is often referred to as 'catch them being good'. That is, the rules are reinforced by actively looking for appropriate behaviour and rewarding it, with the aim of keeping the climate as positive as possible in the classroom.

Even in such a positive climate, problems can obviously arise. Through their general sensitivity to the mood of the class, as well as through their active scanning and monitoring, teachers can be alerted to situations where this might happen. They can also seek to anticipate and avoid unnecessary conflicts. Laslett and Smith (1984) have suggested that the pupils themselves often may not be aware of why they are misbehaving, but they note that minor misdemeanours may escalate into more disruptive incidents unless teachers take prompt action to prevent this. The strategies teachers employ should avoid the sort of threats or disparaging remarks that are likely to back both teachers and pupils into a corner. That is, they must provide a way of 'saving face' for all concerned, if problems are not to escalate. The aim, then, will be to demonstrate that the teacher is in control of, rather than merely reacting to, the situation. It is evident that different strategies will be more successful with some pupils than others, but Laslett and Smith suggest that a

We wish to provide an ethos of mutual respect, self-respect, independence, responsibility and self-motivation.

We believe that good behaviour goes hand in hand with good relationships and that positive rules, negotiated with all concerned and backed by praise and rewards, will help achieve this aim.

Rules, praise and ignoring – guidelines

1 Agree with the class four or five rules and display these on the walls where they can easily be seen. . . .

2 . . . [the rules] should tell the children what they should do rather than what they should not do.

3 Instead of telling them off when they break the rules . . . praise them for keeping to the rules – this may seem somewhat unnatural at first.

4 When you praise them, tell them what it is that they are doing right . . .

5 Use praise more than you normally would to begin with and try to make your praise statements outweigh your telling offs by at least 3 to 1. Make your praise varied and sincere.

6 Try to ignore children who are breaking the rules but praise a child nearby who is keeping to the rules so that the rule breaker can hear you do this. Praise the errant pupil when he/she begins behaving appropriately.

7 If behaviour can't be ignored, remind the child of the rule and give a warning that if it is broken then. . . . (one of the school's agreed sanctions will be applied).

8 Praise this child when he/she begins following the rule again and keep him/her on task by using more praise.

9 If the child ignores the warning . . . (then the agreed sanction is applied).

Figure 6.1. Extracts from an infant school's positive behaviour policy

general principle must be to 'nip trouble in the bud', that is, to move quickly to inhibit any inappropriate behaviour before it becomes more widespread. This is likely to be most effective when it is done in as quiet, good-humoured and matter-of-fact a way as possible. Thus the pupil should be reminded in positive terms of the rules and routines, and be re-directed without more ado to the task in hand.

Figure 6.1 provides extracts from a positive behaviour policy which was developed by the staff of an infant school. As its guidelines on 'rules, praise and ignoring' make clear, there will be times in any classroom when further sanctions or punishments are required. However, following a positive approach to class management, in order to minimize these, the balance of attention should be given to the reinforcement of appropriate conduct. It is worth while considering, therefore, why rewards should be thought to be more effective than punishments. First, what teachers and pupils view as punishments may not correspond. Topping (1983), for example, has reported that frequent verbal reprimand may actually serve to reinforce disruptive behaviour. It might be noted, though, that a similar discrepancy can also occur between teachers and pupils on what constitutes reward: for instance, some pupils may be embarrassed by being singled out for praise in front of their peers. Where such a mismatch exists between teacher intentions and pupil perceptions, the teacher's use of both praise and reprimand may be equally ineffective. A further argument that can be made against the use of punishment is that it acts to focus undue attention on inappropriate behaviour, rather than providing pupils with models of appropriate conduct. Perhaps the strongest concerns, though, relate to the adverse effect that it can have on teacher–pupil relationships. If this is to be minimized, any punishments must be carried out both sensitively and fairly, and also within the framework of a more positive approach. Docking (1989) has emphasized that the focus should be on the reasonableness of the rule that has been infringed, and the teacher's manner should convey that it is the behaviour rather than the pupil that is unacceptable. Further, the reasons for any sanction should be made explicit, and the pupil concerned should be provided with guidance and help to meet the expected standards of behaviour.

Specific strategies for managing problematic behaviour

The emphasis of a positive approach to classroom management is on the prevention of difficult or disruptive behaviour. However, in some cases the extent of a pupil's problematic behaviour will be such as to require more individualized attention. Where this is so it is necessary to gather observational evidence of the nature of the pupil's difficulties in order to determine what sort of intervention might be appropriate. It is important to acknowledge that objective appraisal of behaviour which may be both challenging and undermining of one's confidence can be difficult. It can often be the case that teachers become selectively sensitive to the behaviour of a pupil who gives them cause for concern, and accordingly they may only be alert to his or her inappropriate behaviour rather than to those positive aspects that could be built upon. Further, behaviour which might be ignored in another pupil may be perceived as problematic in that child, and if this leads to overt differences in teachers' reactions, it may serve to reinforce a class perception that the individual, rather than his or her behaviour, is a problem. For these reasons it is helpful to structure one's observations in such a way as to focus systematically on specific aspects of the behaviour that gives concern. One possible framework which has been suggested centres on the following questions: how far does the behaviour interfere with the pupil's learning and that of others? How different is it from the behaviour of others in the class? How often does it occur and how long does it last? From the pupil's point of view, how reasonable is it in the situations in which it occurs? In how many and what sort of situations does it occur? (Leach and Raybould 1977). The answers to questions of this kind should help inform a teacher's assessment of the seriousness of the pupil's difficulties and the need for systematic intervention. They might also provide a basis for discussion and consultation with colleagues, the pupil and the pupil's parents about the appropriate steps that should be taken.

Behavioural strategies

The principles underpinning behavioural strategies are that behaviour which is reinforced tends to be repeated and, conversely, that behaviour which is not reinforced will become less frequent. It should be apparent that these principles are closely associated with a positive approach to general classroom management. It is widely accepted, though, that behavioural approaches can have a very important role to play not only in the establishment of appropriate conduct, but also in the reduction of inappropriate behaviour.

Where pupils show persistent difficulties that cannot be overcome by general management procedures, a structured behavioural approach begins with a detailed observational analysis of incidents of appropriate and inappropriate behaviour. In recording these, particular attention is given to:

(i) the specific situation(s) in which the behaviour occurs;
(ii) the behaviour itself, described in objective and precise terms; and
(iii) the consequences of the behaviour, including both teacher and peer responses.

An analysis of the situations in which different sorts of behaviour are observed may reveal that a pupil's inappropriate behaviour is more likely to occur in some contexts than in others. It might be, for example, that it is more strongly associated with certain pupil groupings than others, or with particular demands such as the sharing of materials. In some cases, this will indicate that minor environmental modifications can be made in order to promote appropriate and inhibit inappropriate behaviour. More generally, though, it will serve to direct a teacher's attention to those contexts which a pupil may find particularly problematic.

The analysis of the consequences of a pupil's behaviour is based on certain assumptions: first, that problem behaviour is being reinforced in the classroom in some way; and conversely, that more appropriate behaviour may be receiving little or no reinforcement. It might be the case, for example, that inappropriate behaviour results in a pupil receiving individual attention, whereas the expected and accepted forms of behaviour are ignored. Where this is so, it could be argued that what are intended by the teacher as reprimands or sanctions actually serve to reinforce misconduct. Such a hypothesis will lead to a plan of action in which the pattern of reinforcement is changed, so that attention is given to appropriate behaviour and withdrawn from unacceptable behaviour. This form of strategy is central to a behavioural approach, for it views acceptable and unacceptable behaviour as essentially incompatible: the increase of one is explicitly linked with the decrease of the other. Any behavioural intervention must therefore aim to increase the incidence of appropriate behaviour and at the same time to reduce the occurrence of problematic behaviour.

In order to increase appropriate behaviour, from this perspective, it may be sufficient to apply the 'catch them being good' strategy, provided that this is done in a consistent and structured way. In some cases, though, there may be few if any occasions when a child can be 'caught being good'. This situation will usually arise where the gap between a pupil's existing behaviour and that which is expected in the classroom is too great to be achievable in one step. Where this is so, it will be necessary to outline the stages through which it might be attained. For example, if a pupil is really 'always' out of his or her seat, then it is likely to be unrealistic to view 'remaining in seat throughout the lesson' as an immediately achievable goal. However, if intermediate goals are planned and discussed with the pupil, he or she will know what to aim for, and can be rewarded for steps along the way which come successively closer to this. In order to be effective, it is important that the pupil not only understands the requirements that are being made, but is also helped to monitor his or her own progress towards the longer term goal. Further, if teacher attention and praise are not found sufficiently rewarding, other forms of reinforcement, such as the privilege of additional time on a preferred activity, will be needed.

Behavioural strategies for decreasing inappropriate behaviour in the classroom will depend upon the analysis of what seems to have been maintaining this. If individual attention, even of a negative kind, has been identified as a contributing factor, then 'planned ignoring' may be used. There are a number of situations in which this is clearly not an appropriate strategy, however, such as in those instances where the ignored behaviour is likely to spread to the pupil's peers, or where the behaviour itself puts the pupil or others at risk. In other circumstances, if planned ignoring is to be effective, it must be consistently applied and should be coupled with the giving of attention for positive behaviour. It should be noted, though, that although it can be an effective strategy, it does often lead to an initial escalation of inappropriate behaviour. Moreover, it will usually require careful explanation, not only to the pupil concerned, but also to others in the class upon whose co-operation its success may depend.

Attention can also be withdrawn from a pupil by the use of 'time out', in which the pupil is removed from the context of general classroom activities to a safe and supervised, but unstimulating, area. In order to be successfully applied, this strategy needs to be fully understood by the pupil, and it should be carried out in a matter-of-fact way and for a brief pre-specified period only, after which the pupil should be welcomed back into classroom activities, with no further discussion of the misbehaviour. It is important to note that this strategy differs in a number of significant ways from the less carefully structured approach of sending children out of the room until the end of a lesson, and reprimanding them subsequently.

The use of 'planned ignoring' will only be effective if teacher and peer attention is perceived as a reinforcement to a pupil. Similarly, 'time out' is likely to be successful only when 'time in' the classroom is rewarding. Where observational analysis has not clearly indicated the influence of teacher or peer attention on a pupil's behaviour, then from a behavioural perspective it follows that it will be necessary to identify other incentives or privileges which can not only be awarded for appropriate behaviour but also withdrawn for inappropriate behaviour. Often this will involve some form of contract between teacher and pupil, and in some situations parental co-operation may also be sought to help implement the strategy.

Whichever strategies are adopted, the behavioural model emphasizes a carefully planned step-by-step approach, in which achievable targets are set at each stage and the pupil is helped to recognize his or her own progress. More detailed discussion of the application of behavioural techniques can be found in a number of sources (e.g. Fontana 1985, Montgomery 1989, Wheldall and Merrett 1984).

Wider approaches

The strengths of the behavioural approach lie in its focus on positive changes which can be achieved within the classroom. It provides a clear structure for observational assessment of the nature of the behaviour causing concern and of the classroom-based factors that may contribute to its occurrence. However, although it provides a valuable resource for teachers, it has some significant limitations if it is used in isolation. The first, and perhaps most obvious, is that it takes no account of the potential effects on a pupil's behaviour not only of the whole school, but also of wider family and community contexts. A recognition of the many interacting factors that may contribute to a pupil's difficulties must imply the need for close liaison between school staff, with parents and, where appropriate, with other agencies, in the development of any classroom-based intervention. Second, children need to be encouraged to monitor and manage their own behaviour, rather than simply to respond to external control. As Docking (1989) has pointed out, whole school policies, class management techniques and behavioural strategies can all be very effective in teaching children to conform to a code of conduct which allows for a stable and secure learning environment. Important though this is, however, he argues that if children are to develop a personal commitment to and sense of responsibility for maintaining particular principles in their behaviour, they need to learn to anticipate and understand the consequences of their own actions, and to acquire sensitivity to the needs and rights of others.

From this perspective then, there is a need to complement behavioural strategies with a more cognitively oriented approach. Cognitive strategies aim to develop the self-regulation of behaviour, by helping children to clarify and assess their own perceptions of problematic situations, and to appraise their strengths and needs in responding to these (e.g. Galvin 1989). Thus the focus is on the full involvement of the pupils themselves in setting aims, planning and evaluating strategies to enhance their behaviour, and recording their own progress. It might be noted that such an approach is not unique to those experiencing emotional or behavioural difficulties. The provision of learning experiences in which pupils are helped to gain increased understanding not only of their own achievements, rights and responsibilities but also those of others is fundamental to personal and social education (Galloway 1990). As the National Curriculum Council has observed, this aspect of the development of all pupils 'cannot be left to chance but needs to be co-ordinated as an explicit part of a school's whole curriculum policy, both inside and outside the formal timetable' (NCC 1989c: para. 10).

Discussion points

1 Outline the rules that you would wish to establish with a class group. Consider how effectively the 'catch them being good' strategy might be applied to reinforce these.
2 A privilege can be given to reward appropriate behaviour, or alternatively it can be withdrawn as a sanction for inappropriate behaviour. Discuss what form privileges might take. In doing so, consider the distinction that should be made between pupils' privileges and pupils' rights. For example, should playtimes be regarded as a privilege which can be withdrawn?
3 Discuss which teaching strategies are likely to be most and least effective in promoting a pupil's sense of personal worth.

Further reading

Galloway, D. (1990) *Pupil Welfare and Counselling*, Harlow: Longman.
Montgomery, D. (1989) *Managing Behaviour Problems*, London: Hodder & Stoughton.

7   Frameworks of support

Throughout the preceding chapters it has been emphasized that all teachers are teachers of pupils with special educational needs, and have a central role not only in their identification and assessment, but also in developing classroom strategies to meet their needs. If teachers are to fulfil this role successfully, however, they need access to advice, support and expertise to supplement and complement their own knowledge and skills. The exact nature of the help available to teachers varies from area to area, but sources of support will include colleagues on the school staff, professionals from outside agencies who work within the school, other professionals who liaise with the school and, finally and importantly, the pupils' parents.

Any network of support is only likely to be effective where there is clear understanding and communication about the complementary roles and responsibilities of all concerned in meeting pupils' needs. In the following discussion it should be borne in mind that support services, and the names given to these, vary from authority to authority, and furthermore that professionals with the same job title may not always approach their work in the same way. Nevertheless, some common features can be described in the pattern of support both within and outside school.

Colleagues on the school staff

Where there is a whole school approach to special educational provision it should follow that many colleagues, including, for example, subject specialists and those with pastoral responsibilities, may provide help and advice in developing strategies to meet individual needs. The number of staff with particular expertise and specific responsibilities in this area will vary according to the size and nature of the school. However, most schools will have a designated member of staff, often referred to as the special needs co-ordinator, whose role it is to develop, co-ordinate and review the provision that is made. Typically, the role will be designed with two aims in mind: not only to arrange and monitor interventions for those pupils who experience learning difficulties, but also to prevent such difficulties from arising unnecessarily.

In relation to the first of these aims, the designated staff member will usually be expected to co-ordinate the identification and assessment of pupils with special educational needs, develop appropriate resource materials, help colleagues plan specific teaching programmes and evaluate their effectiveness, oversee the monitoring of the pupils' progress, and liaise and consult with school staff, support agencies and the pupils' parents. The second aim implies that his or her duties are also likely to include a general brief to raise colleagues' awareness of special educational needs and to work with them to ensure that the curriculum is accessible to all pupils, to contribute to the development of the school's assessment and recording system, and to identify appropriate organizational strategies, time-tabling arrangements and resources to meet the full range of pupils' needs.

It may be seen then that the role incorporates a wide range of liaison and consultancy work including active support of colleagues. The amount of time allocated to direct teaching of pupils will vary in different schools, but co-ordinators and, in larger schools, other special needs teachers, may withdraw individuals or small groups from lessons for specific purposes, as well as offering support within the class. Whatever form such additional assistance takes, it should not be viewed as a means by which class teachers relinquish their responsibility for the pupils' progress. Rather, it is generally agreed that direct support is most successful when the reciprocal roles of class teacher and special needs teacher are acknowledged and clearly defined. It is important, therefore, that the support that is given is based on joint planning, in which both teachers bring their own knowledge and skills to bear.

In some schools, additional help within the classroom will also be provided by ancillary staff. Classroom assistants have traditionally been more associated with primary than secondary schools, but they are being increasingly employed in both settings to support pupils with special educational needs. In a number of LEAs special support assistants are allocated to individual pupils with statements. Although the work that they do is obviously partly determined by the particular pupil's difficulties, it is not unusual to find some lack of clarity about the nature of their role. Too often they have primarily worked in an intensive one-to-one way which effectively segregates the pupil from the rest of the class. However, as discussed in Chapter 5, it is usually found that additional classroom assistance is most effective where it is employed flexibly to support the teacher in meeting the pupil's needs.

LEA support services

Advisory and Support Service

The Warnock Committee (DES 1978) envisaged that, as far as ordinary schools were concerned, the aims of this service should be twofold. That is, first, to develop the general quality of special educational provision by giving advice and support to teachers, and second, to help individual pupils by working with their teachers to overcome learning and behavioural difficulties. Special needs advisers would co-ordinate the work of the service, which would be staffed primarily by advisory teachers and peripatetic specialist teachers. The advisory teachers would work with groups of schools, giving support on the identification of special educational needs and on appropriate methods to meet those needs, as well as providing advice on links with other professionals. The peripatetic specialist teachers would be concerned with the particular needs of children with visual, hearing or physical impairments. Like the advisory teachers, they would work with groups of schools, providing advice and support to the children, their parents and their teachers.

Most LEAs have organized their services along these lines. There is, though, variation in the nature of the support offered to ordinary schools. Further, it should be noted that the full impact of the 1988 Education Act on support services is not yet clear. A recent survey by Moses, Hegarty and Jowett (1988) found that in the majority of LEAs, advisory staff support both individual pupils and teachers, but for most pupils support takes the form of advice to their teachers. It also showed that whereas all LEAs provide ordinary schools with a service for pupils with hearing impairment, rather fewer do so for those with visual impairment. The support for pupils with physical impairment typically takes the form of individually allocated support assistants, although physiotherapy input may be provided by the health authority. Specialist teachers of hearing and visual impairment generally work directly with pupils, liaise with their parents and provide advice to school staff. They often work outside the classroom, where their input is mainly concerned with assessment and monitoring of hearing or vision, provision of aids and the supervision of their use. In addition, they may offer counselling to the pupils. They can provide information for school staff about the nature of a pupil's difficulties, and advice on the use and maintenance of aids. Importantly, they can also give guidance on strategies for the organization of the classroom, and on ways of ensuring access to the curriculum.

Schools Psychological Service

The Schools Psychological Service is staffed by educational psychologists, often working with social workers and specialist teachers. The educational psychologists are extensively involved in statutory assessment procedures: they must contribute to all formal assessments of special educational need and, where statements are maintained for pupils, to their annual reviews and reassessments. They frequently also have the responsibility for collating the assessments made by other professionals and advising the LEA on the type of special educational provision that should be made.

The Warnock Committee saw the role of the Schools Psychological Service as being primarily concerned with individual pupils, and it is certainly the case that individual assessment and programme planning for children with emotional and behavioural or learning difficulties often forms a major part of the work undertaken. Usually, educational psychologists will only be asked for assistance with individual pupils when their needs cannot be met by the school's internal support systems. If appropriate they may work with the pupil's parents as well as with school staff and any other involved professionals, in order to determine strategies for meeting the pupil's needs. In addition to work on individual cases, however, many educational psychologists also undertake a wide range of other activities including INSET (in-service education and training) work with staff groups on issues such as behaviour management, the teaching of social skills, counselling and home–school liaison. In doing so, the aim is to help school staffs develop their own strengths in responding to the full range of their pupils' needs. Accordingly, in some authorities schools are allocated an amount of time from the psychological service, and can negotiate how that time might most effectively be used to meet whole school needs.

Special school staff

The Warnock Committee recommended that all special schools should provide support for teachers in ordinary schools to meet special educational needs and, further, that some should be formally established as resource centres for this purpose. They proposed that such centres could offer guidance and advice on curriculum planning and methods to meet special educational needs, and develop resource materials for use in ordinary schools. Although this recommendation has not always been systematically adopted by LEAs, the majority of special schools have established links of some kind with their neighbourhood schools. Where these are successful, the staffs of both schools can derive valuable support and assistance from one another.

The Educational Welfare Service

Traditionally, the work of educational welfare officers has been mainly concerned with school attendance, but in some authorities they have also played a significant part in supporting children with special educational needs and their families. Their contacts with families may alert them to potential difficulties. They can, therefore, bring to teachers' attention any adverse circumstances in pupils' lives outside school which might affect their learning and behaviour at school. They also represent a valuable link between education and health and social services. With the implementation of the 1989 Children Act, as discussed in the following section, it seems likely that educational welfare officers may take a more prominent and active role in the education of children deemed to be 'in need': a category which includes many of those with special educational needs.

Social services support

Social services departments not only have responsibilities for child care and protection, but are also involved more extensively with both families and wider neighbourhood networks. As a result, they can provide information to schools which is vital in meeting special educational needs, and may in addition help to promote liaison with homes and the local community. The need for more effective collaboration between educational and social services has been recognized for many years, but the arguments have been strengthened and made explicit in the legislation of the 1989 Children Act. Under the definitions of this Act, children are to be regarded as 'in need' if they are 'unlikely to achieve or maintain . . . a reasonable standard of health or development . . . physical, intellectual, emotional, social or behavioural' without the provision of specified services, or if they have substantial and permanent disabilities. A major principle of this Act is that schools and other agencies must work together in close co-operation, and must involve both children and their parents in decisions about the services they provide. Social services departments have a responsibility to inform and consult with LEAs if they have any concerns about the educational welfare of a child. They also have duties to contribute to the provision of services for that child, for example, by providing care or supervised activities outside school hours and during the school holidays. Similarly, LEAs should inform social services departments of their concerns so that, where appropriate, assessments of educational need may be co-ordinated with assessments of wider aspects of need. The whole emphasis of the legislation is that the extent to which any individual child's difficulties hinder his or her development will depend not only on the severity of that difficulty, but also on the support provided at home, in school, and by the various support agencies. It is too early to predict the impact of this Act. However, if authorities fully implement its requirements, it should have an extensive and positive effect on the support that can be provided for those with special educational needs, both in and outside school.

Health authority support

The health visitor service provides an important source of support for families and preschool children at home. Health visitors screen vision, hearing and language development and can alert other services to any indications of particular need. Some have specialized training which equips them to offer direct help to children with specific developmental difficulties or delays and their parents. When children are of school age, school doctors and nurses represent the main source of advice and support on health-related issues and may play an important role in assessing special educational need. In addition to routine screenings and general advice on health education, they will monitor the health of particular pupils, identifying any sources of difficulty and advising on the educational implications of these.

Outside the school context, individual pupils with special educational needs may have contact with a wide range of medical specialists, such as paediatricians, orthopaedic surgeons, neurologists, vision and hearing specialists and so on. Those with significant emotional and or behavioural disturbance may be involved with multidisciplinary child guidance teams, jointly run by the health and education services, and here there is a clear need for close liaison with school staff. This is equally the case when pupils are receiving support from physiotherapists or speech therapists. These therapists typically work in hospitals, clinics and special school settings, although speech therapy and, more rarely, physiotherapy may sometimes be provided in ordinary schools. They are particularly concerned with the assessment and diagnosis of motor or communication difficulties, programme development and the monitoring of individual progress. In addition to their direct involvement with children, they will usually work closely with their parents. It is crucial that they also liaise with their teachers, for they can provide specialist advice on appropriate methods to extend specific skills, as well as information on resources and strategies which can facilitate the children's access to the curriculum.

Reciprocal systems of support

In outlining the main sources of support for pupils with special educational needs the focus so far has been on school and authority services, and it should be noted that these may be complemented by a range of provision which is made by voluntary agencies. Although the emphasis has been placed on the way in which particular colleagues can advise and support teachers to help them meet pupils' needs, it is important to stress that this should not be seen as a one-way process. From their day-to-day interactions with pupils, and from their continuous assessment and monitoring of the effectiveness of different classroom strategies, class teachers gather insights and information which are invaluable to other professionals. If support systems are to be successful in supporting both the pupils and all the staff who work with them, it is essential that the working relationships that this entails are characterized by mutual understanding and respect for the skills, knowledge and expertise that all have to offer. This necessitates an explicit recognition of the complementary roles of all those involved, and of the need for reciprocal support. Furthermore, these perspectives do not only apply to professional networks, but are of equal importance when considering the contribution of parents to their children's education.

Parental support for their children's learning

It has been implicit throughout this book that it is vital that teachers should consult with parents and involve them as fully as possible in their children's education. It is necessary, therefore, to look more explicitly at the question of why parental involvement should merit such an emphasis.

In principle, the importance for schools of seeking to promote positive home–school relationships has long been acknowledged. Since the 1960s a number of governmental reports have addressed the issue, and it was a central theme of the Warnock Committee's recommendations on special educational provision. In a chapter entitled 'Parents as partners' it asserts that:

> the successful education of children with special educational needs is dependent on the full involvement of their parents: indeed, unless the parents are seen as equal partners in the educational process the purpose of our report will be frustrated.
>
> (DES 1978: para. 9.1)

Throughout the educational legislation of the 1980s, there has been a clear focus on the rights of all parents to more detailed information about their children's schooling and progress, and to a certain degree of involvement in decision-making. The 1981 Education Act also specified the ways in which parents should be formally involved in the assessment of special educational need. However, these legal initiatives are not sufficient by themselves to ensure 'full involvement' in the educational process. For example, it is clear from the available evidence that few parents feel they have had any significant influence on decisions made about special educational provision for their children (Sandow et al. 1987, Goacher et al. 1988). Furthermore, it can be argued that the current legislative focus on parents as 'consumers' of the service provided by schools distracts attention from the notion of parent–teacher partnership which Warnock saw as so crucial to successful education.

The rationale for Warnock's position is based on the premise that parents and teachers have complementary skills, knowledge and experiences to bring to children's learning, and that educational progress may best be achieved by actively acknowledging and respecting these. Through the very nature of their role, parents acquire unique knowledge and experience of their own children, and exert a significant influence on all aspects of their development. An extensive body of research literature has described the way in which, from their earliest interactions, parents provide the sorts of stimulation that lay the foundations for subsequent social, emotional, physical and intellectual growth. While many parents may not view their role as one which incorporates systematic teaching, it is evident that a great deal of natural teaching goes on at home before a child starts school. There is no reason to assume that this ceases once formal education begins. Rather, a number of studies (e.g. Tizard *et al.* 1988) have demonstrated that a large proportion of parents also adopt more explicit teaching aims during the primary school years, particularly in relation to literacy and numeracy skills. Perhaps surprisingly, given the weight attributed to homework during secondary school, there is little comparable information on general patterns of parental support of older children. Common sense would suggest that any direct assistance will vary with their children's growing independence as well as with parents' confidence in their own competence to help. However, it seems clear that less direct forms of parental support are likely to remain as a significant influence on learning throughout a child's schooling.

Schools, however, are not always aware of the nature of the help that parents provide at home. Moreover, it is not unusual to find that the contributions of particular parents to their children's education are judged by teachers to be inappropriate, inadequate or deficient in some way. Thus, as Croll and Moses (1985) found, children's learning or behavioural difficulties at school are frequently ascribed in part, if not primarily, to their home circumstances. Where this is so, too often parents may be more readily viewed by schools as 'part of the problem', rather

potential source supp. in prom. prog.

than as a potential source of support in promoting their children's progress.

It is worth considering the evidence upon which such judgements are based. As previously discussed, it has been acknowledged for some time that children from 'lower working-class' backgrounds typically do less well at school, and are more likely to be identified by their teachers as having moderate learning or emotional and behavioural difficulties. Comparative studies of early parent–child interactions have looked for possible explanations in the children's home experiences. Thus, for example, social class differences have been sought and found in child-rearing strategies such as style of language use and attitudes to discipline and control. There is no doubt that a 'child-centred' approach at home is made easier by comfortable material and physical circumstances, and that poverty and oppressive home conditions can have a significant influence on patterns of family interaction. However, it is important to emphasize that more recent studies (e.g. Tizard and Hughes 1984, Wells 1983), while not denying differences between families of different socio-economic status, have described the richness of children's stimulation at home among working-class families. In doing so they provide evidence that seriously challenges the notion that working-class children suffer from linguistic or cognitive deprivation outside school.

The differences in experience that children bring with them when they start school may, however, have a lasting impact on their attainments and behaviour. While one might hope that schools could in some way 'compensate' for assumed or real disadvantage at home, the evidence suggests that this does not often happen. Rather, a number of studies report that, even where children of different social class backgrounds enter school with similar levels of attainment, those from lower working-class families tend to make poorer progress (Mortimore and Blackstone 1982). One explanation for this that is commonly offered is that their parents demonstrate less interest in their education. Undeniably, parental interest, support and encouragement of learning can be crucial factors in children's progress at school. However, it should be noted that there is little evidence to suggest that this is notably lacking among any particular social group as a whole. Some parents will be diffident or lack confidence about what they can contribute to their child's formal education. Others might feel apprehensive in their dealings with schools and the authority that teachers represent. This may particularly be the case for those whose own earlier experiences as pupils at school were poor, and for those whose current contacts are dominated by discussion of the problems rather than the positive achievements of their children. It is important that any such feelings of apprehension are not misjudged as a lack of interest. Unless a school takes active steps to reach out to all parents and to communicate a genuine respect both for their children and themselves, it is unlikely that the full benefits of parental support will be felt.

Although the influence of home and family on children's learning should not be underestimated, neither should that of school. Research into school effectiveness demonstrates that even where the entry skills and home backgrounds of pupils are similar, schools can vary in the standards of educational attainment and behaviour that they achieve. It is evident too that teachers' expectations, the way in which they categorize pupils, their classroom interactions and teaching style can all affect children's learning progress. Some studies have suggested that social class assumptions play a part in the judgements that are made about children at school. That is, teachers may hold different expectations of children from different classes and home backgrounds. It is perhaps inevitable that their assessments will be influenced by the cultural norms with which they are most familiar, but it has frequently been argued that the 'cultural loading' of schools generally favours certain social groups more than others. Certainly, while a 'gap' can be described between the expectations and demands of home and school for all children (e.g. Tizard and Hughes 1984), it is wider for some than for others. Just how far the gap should be bridged is open to debate, but at the very least it seems essential that teachers should not make assumptions about their pupils' home backgrounds. In order to avoid this, teachers require accurate information and insights into children's learning experiences outside school. The implication, therefore, is that teachers need to seek ways to establish effective methods of communication with pupils' parents.

Constructive two-way communication between home and school has been identified as one of the factors associated with effective education at both primary and secondary levels (Mortimore *et al.* 1988, ILEA 1984). If good parent–teacher relationships are to be established, this requires positive attitudes from staff and a considerable whole school commitment to the time and effort that may be involved. Given the pressures of competing priorities in schools, therefore, it is important to explore the evidence for the view that parents might be willing to become involved more closely in their children's education and, furthermore, that this would lead to enhanced progress.

In the preschool years, if their children have significantly delayed development, it is frequently reported that most parents wish for practical guidance and support on how they might best promote their children's learning (Mittler and Mittler 1982). This is fortunate from a professional point of view, because research into early intervention schemes suggests that their effectiveness is likely to be sustained and enhanced where parents are actively involved (e.g. Lazar and Darlington 1982). Accordingly, parental involvement is usually now seen as an essential component of such schemes. Since the 1981 Act, a home-based service which relies on parents as the primary teachers of their children has become a predominant form of early provision for children with special educational needs. This service is based on the Portage model (White and Cameron 1987). The exact form it takes can vary from authority to authority, but where it has been evaluated there is evidence that both children and parents benefit from their involvement (Daly *et al.* 1985). It seems probable that many parents who have experienced a Portage service will seek to continue their teaching role in some way once their children begin school. In recognition of this, some authorities have extended their schemes into primary schools, where parents and teachers work together on individual educational programmes.

For most parents, however, their children's special educational needs are only identified at some stage during formal schooling. Their readiness to work together with the school will clearly be influenced not only by their existing relationship with the staff, but also by the manner in which they are alerted to the causes for concern. Where the parents' perception is that their views are not listened to, that their own assessment of their child's needs is judged less valid than those of the teachers, or that they are implicitly criticized, it is not surprising if they are unenthusiastic. On the other hand, if teachers are open and demonstrate that they value the parents' perspectives and insights, and respect the contribution they make to support their child's learning, one might predict a more positive response. Certainly, the evidence from well-planned schemes to involve parents in the teaching of reading suggests that there is a great deal of willingness among parents to work with teachers to help their children.

Most children with special educational needs experience difficulties in their reading, and it is in this area of the curriculum that there is the most powerful evidence for the benefits of parent–teacher collaboration. Hewison and her colleagues found that among children from working-class backgrounds, levels of reading attainment were strongly associated with whether their mothers regularly listened to them reading at home (Hewison and Tizard 1980). On the basis of this finding, they initiated a major intervention study known as the Haringey project, which aimed to explore whether it could be demonstrated that such parental help led to enhanced achievements for their children. Parents of six-year-old children were asked to hear their children read on a regular basis over a two-year period. Most not only agreed to do so, but also maintained a high level of commitment to the project throughout the two years. Their children's reading attainments were monitored and compared with those of two other groups of pupils. The first of these were given regular input at school by a specialist teacher of reading. The second received no additional help other than that which was normally provided by their class teachers. The results showed that children in the parental involvement group made significant and lasting gains in comparison with the others. Additionally, teachers and parents spoke of wider benefits to the children's progress at school, and of their satisfaction with the improved home–school relationships which had been developed (Tizard, Schofield and Hewison 1982).

Not surprisingly, this study gave a considerable impetus to other schemes which sought to promote parental involvement in reading. A wide variety of approaches has been adopted and, while not all have been rigorously evaluated, gains have been described both in children's reading skills and also in their general approach to learning and behaviour at school (Topping and Wolfendale 1985). Increasingly, therefore, as schools become more convinced of the benefits, and more confident in their approach, parental involvement schemes have been developed not only in other aspects of the curriculum such as mathematics, but, equally importantly, in the area of behaviour management (Topping 1986). The extent of planned and active parental involvement varies in different areas of the country, and is more associated with primary than secondary education. However, over the last decade there has been an evident growth of these schemes in all sectors of the school system (Jowett *et al.* 1991). Some are specifically focused on children with special educational needs, particularly at secondary level, but an underlying principle during the earlier years of school appears to be that many potential areas of difficulty might be prevented if parents can be fully involved.

There is, then, a strong educational rationale for promoting positive approaches to parent–teacher collaboration. However, it should be noted that the parental involvement schemes described above do not necessarily represent the type of partnership between home and school that the Warnock Committee discussed. Typically, parents are involved on the school's terms, and there may be little explicit attempt to take their priorities and perspectives into account when developing the approach that is followed. Thus, it is quite possible for teachers to participate in a scheme without acknowledging the skills, knowledge and insights that parents might contribute. Furthermore, if active collaboration of this kind is seen as the major way in which parents can be involved in their children's education, this can distract attention from those who are unable or unwilling to take part. There is no doubt that where parents and teachers work together with a positive focus on children's learning and development, this can do much to enhance home–school relationships. However, if these relationships are to be established on a basis of mutual trust and respect, there is a need for a flexible system of genuine two-way communication which goes far wider than only asking parents to take part in programmes of work designed by the school.

Partnership, as envisaged in the Warnock Report, involves a full sharing of the unique expertise parents have in relation to their own children with the wider educational expertise of teachers and other professionals. From this perspective, parents must be seen as key participants in assessment and decision-making about provision to meet their children's educational needs. If such a relationship is to be developed, positive attitudes on both sides are clearly fundamental. Schools can do a great deal to promote these. A necessary starting point is an agreed whole school policy which aims to demonstrate that the staff both recognize and value the support that parents have to offer. Partnership has frequently been described as an ideal rather than an attainable goal. Certainly, as Sandow and her colleagues (1987) have observed, it is as yet a term far more readily used by professionals than parents when referring to home–school interactions. Nevertheless, there is no doubt that it is a goal for which it is worth striving. Parents represent a potentially very powerful resource in the education of all children. The greater the level of a child's educational need, the more important it is that all available resources are brought together in order to meet this. There are strong grounds for the argument that special educational needs can best be met where teachers and parents aim to establish a relationship of reciprocal support.

Discussion points

1 Extra support in school for pupils with special educational needs is most effective where it is based on joint planning between class teacher and support teacher. In order to explore why this might be so, consider (i) the knowledge and skills that class teachers can contribute to joint planning; and (ii) the ways in which they might best draw on specialist help to

support their own approach to meeting pupils' needs.

2 Discuss the areas of overlap and the boundaries between the roles and responsibilities of parents and teachers in children's education. To what extent can their roles be seen as complementary?

3 What would you see as the main rationale for home–school partnership? Consider the challenges that the notion of partnership presents for teachers, and the extent to which it might be viewed as an achievable goal.

Further reading

Bastiani, J. (ed.) (1988) *Parents and Teachers 2: From Policy to Practice*, Windsor: NFER-Nelson.

Davies, J. D. and Davies, P. (eds) (1989) *A Teacher's Guide to Support Services*, Windsor: NFER-Nelson.

Sources of further information

Related to the full range of special educational needs

The National Association for Special Educational Needs (NASEN), York House, Exhall Grange, Wheelwright Lane, Coventry CV7 9HP. This association, which has recently been formed by the amalgamation of two former organizations (NCSE and NARE), publishes two journals concerning educational provision for pupils with special educational needs: the *British Journal of Special Education* and *Support for Learning*.

An independent magazine, *Special Children*, which is aimed at parents, teachers and others concerned with special educational needs is based at 73 All Saints Road, Kings Heath, Birmingham B14 7LN.

Publications and information sheets regarding integration in ordinary schools are produced by the Centre for Studies on Integration in Education (CSIE), at 415 Edgware Road, London NW2 6NB.

Related to specific forms of special educational needs

There are many voluntary organizations which bring together children, parents and professionals with a specific focus on a particular form of special educational need. The following selective list, in alphabetical order, draws attention to some of those that can provide information and guidance for teachers.

AFASIC (The Association for All Speech Impaired Children), 347 Central Markets, Smithfield, London EC1A 9NH.

Association for Spina Bifida and Hydrocephalus, 42 Park Road, Peterborough PE1 2UQ.

British Dyslexia Association, 98 London Road, Reading RG1 5AU.

Down's Syndrome Association, Mitcham Road, London SW17 9PG.

In Touch, 10 Norman Road, Sale M33 3DF. (Provides a newsletter with information and contacts, particularly for parents of children with rare or complex impairments.)

MENCAP (The Royal Society for Mentally Handicapped Children and Adults), 123 Golden Lane, London EC1 0RT.

National Deaf Children's Society, Family Service Centre, 24 Wakefield Road, Rothwell Haigh, Leeds LS26 0SF.

National Society for Autistic Children, 1A Golders Green Road, London N7.

RNIB (The Royal National Institute for the Blind), 224 Great Portland Street, London WIN 6AA.

RNID (The Royal National Institute for the Deaf), 105 Gower Street, London WC1 6AH.

The Spastics Society, 12 Park Crescent, London WIN 4EQ.

References

Ainscow, M. (1989) 'How should we respond to individual needs?', in M. Ainscow and A. Florek (eds) *Special Educational Needs: Towards a Whole School Approach*, London: David Fulton.

Ainscow, M. and Muncey, J. (1989) *Meeting Individual Needs*, London: David Fulton.

Ainscow, M. and Tweddle, D. (1979) *Preventing Classroom Failure: An Objectives Approach*, London: Wiley.

Ainscow, M. and Tweddle, D. (1984) *Early Learning Skills Analysis*, London: Wiley.

Ainscow, M. and Tweddle, D. A. (1988) *Encouraging Classroom Success*, London: David Fulton.

Barnes, D. (1982) *Practical Curriculum Study*, London: Routledge & Kegan Paul.

Bastiani, J. (ed.) (1988) *Parents and Teachers 2: From Policy to Practice*, Windsor: NFER-Nelson.

Bearison, D. J. (1983) 'New directions in studies of social interaction and cognitive growth', in F. C. Serafica (ed.) *Social-Cognitive Development in Context*, London: Methuen.

Bishop, J. and Gregory, S. (1986) 'Hearing impairment', in B. Gillham (ed.) *Handicapping Conditions in Childhood*, London: Croom Helm.

Brennan, W. K. (1985) *Curriculum for Special Needs*, Milton Keynes: Open University Press.

Buckley, S. (1985) 'Teaching parents to teach reading to teach language: a project with Down's syndrome children and their parents', in K. J. Topping and S. Wolfendale (eds) *Parental Involvement in Children's Reading*, London: Croom Helm.

Chapman, E. K. and Stone, J. M. (1988) *The Visually Handi-*

capped Child in Your Classroom, London: Cassell.
Clunies-Ross, L. and Wimhurst, S. (1983) *The Right Balance: Provision for Slow Learners in Secondary Schools*, Windsor: NFER-Nelson.
Cole, T. (1989) *Apart or A Part? Integration and the Growth of British Special Education*, Milton Keynes: Open University Press.
Croll, P. and Moses, D. (1985) *One in Five: The Assessment and Incidence of Special Educational Needs*, London: Routledge & Kegan Paul.
Cunningham, C. (1988) *Down's Syndrome: An Introduction for Parents*, London: Souvenir Press.
Daly, B., Addingham, J., Kerfoot, S. and Sigston, A. (eds) (1985) *Portage: the Importance of Parents*, Windsor: NFER-Nelson.
Daniels, H. and Ware, J. (eds) (1990) *Special Educational Needs and the National Curriculum*, Bedford Way Series, London: Kogan Page.
Davies, J. D. and Davies, P. (eds) (1989) *A Teacher's Guide to Support Services*, Windsor: NFER-Nelson.
Dawkins, J. (1991) *Models of Mainstreaming for Visually Impaired Pupils*, London: HMSO.
DES (1978) *Special Educational Needs* (The Warnock Report), Cmnd 7212, London: HMSO.
DES (1981) *Education Act (1981)*, London: HMSO.
DES (1983a) *Circular 1/83: Assessments and Statements of Special Educational Needs: Procedures within the Education, Health and Social Services*, London: DES.
DES (1983b) *Education (Special Educational Needs) Regulations 1983*, S.I. 1983 no. 29, London: HMSO.
DES (1988) *Education Reform Act (1988)*, London: HMSO.
DES (1989a) *Circular 6/89: The Education Reform Act 1988: National Curriculum: Mathematics and Science Orders under Section 4*, London: DES.
DES (1989b) *Circular 22/89: Assessments and Statements of Special Educational Needs: Procedures within the Education, Health and Social Services*, London: DES.
DES (1989c) *Discipline in Schools* (The Elton Report), London: HMSO.
Dessent, T. (1987) *Making the Ordinary School Special*, Lewes:

Falmer.

Docking, J. (1989) 'The Good Behaviour Guide: HMI observations on school discipline', in N. Jones (ed.) *Special Educational Needs Review Vol. 1*, Lewes: Falmer.

Fish, J. (1989) *What is Special Education?*, Milton Keynes: Open University Press.

Fontana, D. (1985) *Classroom Control: Understanding and Guiding Classroom Behaviour*, London: BPS/Methuen.

Frith, U. (1989) *Autism*, Oxford: Blackwell.

Galloway, D. (1985) *Schools, Pupils and Special Educational Needs*, London: Croom Helm.

Galloway, D. (1990) *Pupil Welfare and Counselling*, Harlow: Longman.

Galvin, P. (1989) 'Behaviour problems and cognitive processes', in D. A. Sugden (ed.) *Cognitive Approaches in Special Education*, Lewes: Falmer.

Galvin, P., Mercer, S. and Costa, P. (1990) *Building a Better Behaved School*, York: Longman.

Gipps, C., Gross, H. and Goldstein, H. (1987) *Warnock's Eighteen Per Cent*, Lewes: Falmer.

Goacher, B., Evans, J., Welton, J. and Wedell, K. (1988) *Policy and Provision for Special Educational Needs: Implementing the 1981 Education Act*, London: Cassell.

Goddard, A. (1983) 'Processes in special education', in G. Blenkin and V. Kelly (eds) *The Primary Curriculum in Action*, London: Harper & Row.

Gulliford, R. (1985) *Teaching Children with Learning Difficulties*, Windsor: NFER-Nelson.

Hegarty, S., Pocklington, K. and Lucas, D. (1981) *Educating Pupils with Special Needs in the Ordinary School*, Windsor: NFER-Nelson.

Henderson, S. and Sugden, D. (1991) 'Pupils with motor impairment', in National Children's Bureau, *Signposts to Special Needs*, Nottingham: NES Arnold.

Hewison, J. and Tizard, J. (1980) 'Parental involvement and reading attainment', *British Journal of Educational Psychology* 50: 209–15.

HMI (1989) *A Survey of Pupils with Special Educational Needs in Ordinary Schools 1988–1989*, London: DES.

HMI (1991) *National Curriculum and Special Needs*, London: DES.

Hodgson, A. (1989) 'Meeting special needs in mainstream classrooms', in M. Ainscow and A. Florek (eds) *Special Educational Needs: Towards a Whole School Approach*, London: David Fulton.

House of Commons Select Committee (1987) *Special Educational Needs: Implementation of the 1981 Education Act*, London: HMSO.

ILEA (1984) *Improving Secondary Schools* (The Hargreaves Report), London: ILEA.

ILEA (1985) *Educational Opportunities for All?* (The Fish Report), London: ILEA.

Jones, N. J. (1983) 'An integrative approach to special educational needs', *Forum* 25 (2): 36–9.

Jowett, S., Baginsky, M. and McNeill, M. M. (1991) *Building Bridges: Parental Involvement in Schools*, Windsor: NFER-Nelson.

Jowett, S., Hegarty, S. and Moses, D. (1988) *Joining Forces: A Study of Links between Special and Ordinary Schools*, Windsor: NFER-Nelson.

Laslett, R. and Smith, C. (1984) *Effective Classroom Management*, London: Croom Helm.

Lazar, I. and Darlington, R. (1982) 'Lasting effects of early education: a report from the consortium for longitudinal studies', *Monographs of the Society for Research in Child Development* 46, serial no. 190.

Leach, D. J. and Raybould, E. C. (1977) *Learning and Behaviour Difficulties in School*, London: Open Books.

Lewis, A. (1991) *Primary Special Needs and the National Curriculum*, London: Routledge.

Lunt, I. (1990) 'Local management of schools and education', in H. Daniels and J. Ware (eds) *Special Educational Needs and the National Curriculum*, Bedford Way Series, London: Kogan Page.

Mittler, P. and Farrell, P. (1987) 'Can children with severe learning difficulties be educated in ordinary schools?', *European Journal of Special Needs Education* 2: 221–36.

Mittler, P. and Mittler, H. (1982) *Partnership with Parents*,

Stratford upon Avon: National Council for Special Education.

Montgomery, D. (1989) *Managing Behaviour Problems*, London: Hodder & Stoughton.

Mortimore, J. and Blackstone, T. (1982) *Disadvantage and Education*, London: Heinemann.

Mortimore, P., Sammons, P., Stoll, L., Lewis, D. and Ecob, R. (1988) *School Matters*, London: Open Books.

Moses, D., Hegarty, S. and Jowett, S. (1988) *Supporting Ordinary Schools: LEA Initiatives*, Windsor: NFER-Nelson.

National Children's Bureau (1991) *Signposts to Special Needs*, Nottingham: NES Arnold.

NCC (1989a) *Circular No. 5. Implementing the National Curriculum – Participation by Pupils with Special Educational Needs*, York: NCC.

NCC (1989b) *Curriculum Guidance 2. A Curriculum for All*, York: NCC.

NCC (1989c) *Circular No. 6. The National Curriculum and Whole Curriculum Planning: Preliminary Guidance*, York: NCC.

Norwich, B. (1990) *Reappraising Special Needs Education*, London: Cassell.

Pollard, A. (1988) 'The social context of special needs in classrooms', in G. Thomas and A. Feiler (eds) *Planning for Special Needs: A Whole School Approach*, Oxford: Blackwell.

Pyke, N. (1991) 'Queues for special help grow longer', *Times Educational Supplement*, 22 March.

Ramasut, A. (ed.) (1989) *Whole School Approaches to Special Needs: A Practical Guide for Secondary Teachers*, Lewes: Falmer.

Roaf, C. (1989) 'Developing whole school policy: a secondary school perspective', in C. Roaf and H. Bines (eds) *Needs, Rights and Opportunities: Developing Approaches to Special Education*, Lewes: Falmer.

Roaf, C. and Bines, H. (eds) (1989) *Needs, Rights and Opportunities: Developing Approaches to Special Education*, Lewes: Falmer.

Rutter, M., Maugham, B., Mortimore, P., Ouston, J. and Smith, A. (1979) *Fifteen Thousand Hours: Secondary Schools and Their Effects on Pupils*, London: Open Books.

Sandow, S., Stafford, D. and Stafford, P. (1987) *An Agreed Understanding? Parent–professional communication and the 1981 Education Act*, Windsor: NFER-Nelson.

SEAC (1989) *Recorder No. 5*, London: SEAC.

SEAC (1990) *A Guide to Teacher Assessment*, London: SEAC/ Heinemann.

Solity, J. and Bull, S. (1987) *Special Needs: Bridging the Curriculum Gap*, Milton Keynes: Open University Press.

Stenhouse, L. (1975) *An Introduction to Curriculum Research and Development*, London: Heinemann.

Sugden, D., Beveridge, S., Burns, J., Drizi, A., Rose, C. and Shepherd, M. (1989) *Leeds Education Authority Special Educational Needs Support Programme in Middle and High Schools: Evaluation Report 1*, Leeds: University of Leeds.

Swann, W. (1988a) 'Integration? Look twice at statistics', *British Journal of Special Education* 15: 102.

Swann, W. (1988b) 'Learning difficulties and curriculum reform: integration or differentiation?', in G. Thomas and A. Feiler (eds) *Planning for Special Needs: A Whole School Approach*, Oxford: Blackwell.

Thomas, G. and Feiler, A. (eds) (1988) *Planning for Special Needs: A Whole School Approach*, Oxford: Blackwell.

Tizard, B., Blatchford, P., Burke, J., Farquhar, C. and Plewis, I. (1988) *Young Children at School in the Inner City*, London: Lawrence Erlbaum.

Tizard, B. and Hughes, M. (1984) *Young Children Learning*, London: Fontana.

Tizard, J., Schofield, W. N. and Hewison, J. (1982) 'Collaboration between teachers and parents in assisting children's reading', *British Journal of Educational Psychology*, 52: 1–15.

Tomlinson, S. (1981) 'The social construction of the ESN(M) child', in L. Barton and S. Tomlinson (eds) *Special Education: Policies, Practices and Social Issues*, London: Harper & Row.

Tomlinson, S. (1982) *A Sociology of Special Education*, London: Routledge & Kegan Paul.

Topping, K. (1983) *Educational Systems for Disruptive Adolescents*, London: Croom Helm.

Topping, K. (1986) *Parents as Educators: Training Parents to Teach Their Children*, London: Croom Helm.

Topping, K. (1988) *The Peer Tutoring Handbook*, London: Croom Helm.

Topping, K. and Wolfendale, S. (eds) (1985) *Parental Involvement in Children's Reading*, London: Croom Helm.

Tyler, R. W. (1949) *Basic Principles of Curriculum and Instruction*, Chicago: Chicago University Press.

Tyre, C. and Young, P. (1991) 'Pupils with specific learning difficulties', in National Children's Bureau, *Signposts to Special Needs*, Nottingham: NES Arnold.

Upton, G. (1990) 'The Education Reform Act and special educational needs', *Association of Child Psychology and Psychiatry Newsletter* 12 (5): 3–8.

Vaughan, M. (1989) 'Parents, children and the legal framework', in C. Roaf and H. Bines (eds) *Needs, Rights and Opportunities: Developing Approaches to Special Education*, Lewes: Falmer.

Webster, A. and McConnell, C. (1987) *Children with Speech and Language Disorders*, London: Cassell.

Webster, A. and Wood, D. J. (1989) *Children with Hearing Difficulties*, London: Cassell.

Wedell, K. (1990) 'Overview: the 1988 Act and current principles of special educational needs', in H. Daniels and J. Ware (eds) *Special Educational Needs and the National Curriculum*, Bedford Way Series, London: Kogan Page.

Wells, G. (1983) 'Talking with children: the complementary roles of parents and teachers', in M. Donaldson, R. Grieve and C. Pratt (eds) *Early Childhood Development and Education*, Oxford: Blackwell.

Welton, J. (1989) 'Incrementalism to catastrophe theory: policy for children with special educational needs', in C. Roaf and H. Bines (eds) *Needs, Rights and Opportunities: Developing Approaches to Special Education*, Lewes: Falmer.

Welton, J., Wedell, K. and Vorhaus, G. (1982) *Meeting Special Educational Needs: The 1981 Act and its Implications*, Bedford Way Paper No. 12, London: Heinemann.

Westwood, P. (1987) *Commonsense Methods for Children with Special Needs*, London: Croom Helm.

Wheldall, K. and Merrett, F. (1984) *Positive Teaching: The Behavioural Approach*, London: Allen & Unwin.

White, M. and Cameron, S. (1987) *The Portage Early Education Programme*, Windsor: NFER-Nelson.

Wolfendale, S. (1987) *Primary Schools and Special Needs: Policy, Planning and Provision*, London: Cassell.

Index

relationships with pupils 96–9;
role in identification and
assessment 46–50, 73–7,
99–100

visual impairment 39–40

Warnock report: concept of
special educational need 2–6;
continuum of special
educational provision 15, 51;
identification and assessment
of need 15; integration 52;
partnership with parents 15,
21, 77, 114–15, 121; support
services 108–10

whole school approach: to special
educational need 25–6, 29,
57–8, 87–8, 106–7; to positive
behaviour 95–6, 98

withdrawal sessions 87–9